ADVANCE PRAISE

"This is the best book I have yet seen to help heal relationships with our bodies! Farnsworth takes her reader step-by-step through various life difficulties and suggests ways and tools for choosing very practical and achievable paths to good solutions. She does so with a touching warmth and understanding."
– Lydia Salant, MA., LicAc., Psychic Therapist

JANET FARNSWORTH, MSW

LOVE

YOUR

BODY

THE GUIDE TO STOP MAKING YOUR BODY A BATTLEGROUND

LOVE YOUR BODY
THE ULTIMATE GUIDE TO STOP MAKING
YOUR BODY A BATTLEGROUND

Difference Press, Washington, D.C., USA
© Janet Farnsworth, 2019

ISBN: 978-1-68309-260-5

Cover Design: Jennifer Stimson
Editor: Cory Hott
Author Photo Courtesy of: Madeleine Tilin Photography

DP
DIFFERENCE PRESS

To Love.
Because I know I can find you in my children's
faces, friendships, clients, sunshine and skin, and in
every place where I was sure you abandoned me,
but just needed to look.

TABLE OF CONTENTS

CHAPTER 1   My Body Is a Battleground   9

CHAPTER 2   It Feels Like Dying   25

CHAPTER 3   There Is a Way!   35

CHAPTER 4   You First   49

CHAPTER 5   Your Extraordinary, Ordinary Biology   67

CHAPTER 6   (The Art of) Feeling   83

CHAPTER 7   Your Body   101

CHAPTER 8   Your Awakening   117

CHAPTER 9   Your Intuition   137

CHAPTER 10 Let Love Move You   149

CHAPTER 11 Obstacles   165

CHAPTER 12 Abundance Ahead   183

Acknowledgments   189

Thank You   193

About the Author   195

About Difference Press   197

Other Books by Difference Press   199

CHAPTER 1

MY BODY IS A BATTLEGROUND

Did you look in the mirror today? Did you fix your hair or brush your teeth? Do you remember what you said to yourself when you looked?

Was it a loud voice? Or maybe a whisper? Did you track the list of things you were unhappy with or wanted to change? Or were the voices mute, utterly resigned to never seeing or looking the way you believe you should?

How about when you got dressed? Did you pick something to wear that made you look "better" (thinner, taller, older, younger, sexier, more serious) than what you saw in the mirror? Were your clothes actually comfortable?

It is not just your appearance; it is also how your body feels – sitting, moving, or being with other people. Maybe it is a feeling of discomfort; maybe it is not feeling at all, but a disconnection.

How about intimate relationships? How does it feel to be seen (literally)? Or to be touched? Is there that one spot you must keep secret?

Most women have at least one private, secret shame with their bodies.

A *Daily Mail* survey of more than 45,000 women (July 2019) found that almost sixty percent said they "hate" the way they look. A 2018 article in Psych-Central estimated that eighty percent of women are "dissatisfied" with their appearance, while *Glamour* magazine conducted a survey and found ninety-seven percent of women dislike their bodies.

And it is not just women. A 2016 survey by Girl Guides UK found that forty percent of seven- to ten-year-olds sometimes felt ashamed or embarrassed about their bodies. Seven years old and embarrassed!

You have been struggling with your body for a very long time. Too long.

Some of that is self-inflicted; some of it is social. One study found ninety-four percent of all teenage girls and sixty-four percent of teenage boys have been shamed for the way their bodies look.

And then there is the ever-present judge ready to evaluate or condemn. Even when you are feeling strong or sexy or maybe even just relaxed, there is that inevitable impulse to improve.

What is worse, you know that somehow you are "supposed" to be accepting of yourself and utterly at ease with how and who you are. It is impossible to pick up any magazine or scroll through any feed and avoid being told to "love yourself" (all while being confronted with images of perfection). One 2015 SELF study reported that eighty-five percent of women believe they should feel more body-positive than they do – meaning, you hate your body and now also hate your-self for feeling that way.

But how do you love yourself when that elusive, "perfect" body is so specific and you are much more complicated?

When you are on the treadmill of "self-improve-ment," how can you ever appreciate the self you actu-ally have?

It is an exhausting, unfair, and unreasonable expec-tation you have been forced to buy into.

I lived through a brief stint with anorexia in high school, followed by mild obesity in college.

The idea of just being myself as I was – "overweight," insecure, and afraid – was reason enough to make sure I wasn't.

To compensate, I went through a stage after col-lege of thinking my most confident self should wear high boots, black clothes, and fishnet stockings (think: 1980's Madonna). I figured that if I looked right (well, at least looked like her) then I could get other peo-ple to find me attractive and then maybe I would find myself attractive. It sort of worked.

Linda is a thirty-two-year old business executive who couldn't walk by a mirror without staring at her stomach and thinking, "I am so fat." She inevitably would pull her belly in and start to think about what she ate, what she could eat, and all the things she wanted to eat but wouldn't.

Jane is fifty-one and managed to get ready for work without actually looking in the mirror at all. She knew that if she did, all she would see were wrinkles, eye bags, and spots.

Laquisha, a twenty-eight-year old athlete, only wore clothes with Spanx to make sure any trace of cellulite she had did not show.

Jarna is sixty-four and was so at war with her body that she scratched her arms until they bled and she had to bandage them.

All of these women knew the agony of body shame and the ways it impacted the quality of their lives. The self-blame and self-dissatisfaction expressed in "harmless" ways, like Madonna hair, or more painful ways, like self-mutilation.

The suffering did just stop at appearance. That was only the first layer. Below and through it were stories of impacted relationships, work, and life choices.

The likelihood is you are fighting with some aspect of yourself or are feeling some sort of betrayal by your body.

You are saturated everywhere with the impossible goal of accepting – even loving – your body when you have almost no opportunity to come to terms with how your body actually is.

You have a hundred ways to hide or "improve" but so few (if any) ways to find genuine pleasure with the body you are in.

If you have ever felt unhappy with or betrayed by your body – and guess what, most of us have – this book is for you.

"I FEEL LIKE THERE IS A HOLE WHERE I SHOULD BE"

When I first met Amy, she was forty-one. Slight of build, with black hair and a worried expression, she came to my office because she felt desperate about the state of her partnership.

She reported extreme anxiety and had a great deal of pain in her stomach and chest. Most distressingly for her, she became increasingly intolerant of her husband Jake's touch, and in fact, found even the idea of sex to be unpleasant.

But she loved him and believed that it was important to her marriage to be physically intimate. She also wanted to keep Jake happy, who had made it known in the nicest way he could that while she had lost interest he most definitely had not. So to "rev up" her sex drive and compensate for her disinterest, she tried everything she could think of: hot baths, silk nightgowns, wine, and hot milk. She read all the "how to love your man" books and listened to podcasts on sex. Anything to make her feel more "turned on."

But the truth was that any time her husband Jake even got near, she wanted to scream. She loved him, but just didn't want him anywhere close.

Because of this, she wasn't sleeping well and would often lie awake at night trying to relax while lying next to Jake. Instead of sex or sleep, her bed became a place to worry about feeling like she was failing as a wife.

With a full-time job, two kids at home, and no sleep, Amy felt like she was at the end of her rope.

More than anything, Amy wanted to worry less, enjoy sex more, and feel like a good spouse.

She had a vague idea that if she could feel better in her body, maybe the other problems would go away. She came to me for somatic therapy, a practice which looks at traditional therapy issues and says that both the suffering and the answers can be found in the body.

When I met with her, we explored the pain in her belly as our starting point.

Amy identified a feeling that no matter how much food she ate, how much wine she drank, how many of her kids' games, concerts, and classes she visited, or how often she spent time with her husband, she felt empty.

As we sat together and explored the empty feeling, she identified a deep hunger – a pervasive ache that felt as if it could never be satisfied. Somewhere in her gut, like a gaping hole, or sometimes she said, like a chainsaw below her bellybutton, nothing fed it.

"I feel like there is a hole where I should be," she said.

Amy's body had become her battleground.

When you love someone in an intimate way, you want to feel close. You want to feel connected and seen. You want to know that you are safe with them and can rest in their arms. But what about when their arms are not a place you want to be?

What about when the way two people traditionally get close – through intimate, physical contact – has become instead a way to feel further apart?

It is a torture.

It wore Amy down and made her miserable. She was losing interest in almost everything, and she felt like she was missing out on what she believed could be a happy time of her life: She wanted to enjoy her relationship. She wanted to want touch. She wanted to want sex.

But she didn't know how.

I know how that feels – wanting the answers but not knowing how to get them.

And so do you because you are holding this book.

You may feel something similar, and I am so sorry things are hard right now. It is an agony – this wanting what you cannot seem to get.

You want to stop blaming your body and feeling like it is a battleground.

You want to be able to get dressed and undressed and not hear the relentless voice of criticism.

You want to enjoy what, for many, is the best of partnership and welcome touch and intimacy.

You want your body to be a source of pleasure rather than unhappiness.

My God, you just want to feel comfortable with your own arms, legs, face, hips, flesh, and fatty places. Please!

The good news is that you can.

This book introduces you to a body-centered practice called The Practice of Now: Let Love Move You (PON). A seven-step process, PON transforms your relationship with your body as it is right now – from dissatisfied, frustrated and disconnected – to easy, nourishing, and soul satisfied.

Kathy was a thirty-eight-year-old single mother who came to me because she wanted to be in a relationship. In recovery from addiction, she had already done many years of personal growth and exploration and believed she was ready to find her life partner.

When she came to me, she was convinced the only way to find her life partner – by being the woman she thought she should be – was if she lost fifteen pounds. Two years earlier, she lost twenty pounds but wanted to lose more. She suspected there was trauma stored in her body which was keeping her from losing the final weight. So she sought me, a body-centered psychotherapist, for treatment.

In the Practice of Now, you start where you are, rather than make plans for where you want to be.

So Kathy began with her longing to lose weight.

"Where do you feel the longing, Kathy?'

"I can feel it in my chest and in my gut mostly. It's like an ache."

She practiced paying attention to the feeling and became more acquainted, even intimate with it – its colors, shapes, sounds, even language. It was brown and jagged and made a kind of guttural groan. The words, when they came, where staccato, and sounded something like "must. have. help." As she listened to her body, she became aware of a second voice, one which was more insistent, shrill, and cruel sounding. Its words were more "you ugly pig.

You piece of trash." Its colors were red and black.

This was how she came to understand her desire to lose weight.

After some time together, we discussed her history of abuse and the father who bullied her as a child.

Without analyzing but simply allowing, she paused and described the way she felt about him while he taunted her.

The feeling was red and black and insistent, shrill, and cruel sounding. The words here, while not quite the same, were close: "you pig. You piece of trash."

Almost immediately, she identified – not interpreted – the feeling as a match with her longing to lose weight. This was not an intellectual match; it was purely somatic.

Now Kathy was at the feeling behind the feeling, and she could do the work of attending to the roots of her relationship with her body as it was.

With time, Kathy pieced together and understood her desire to lose the weight with anger she had not yet expressed – and ironically, how keeping the weight was one way to let herself still feel the rage she had never been able to show her father.

In Kathy's case, when she recognized and cared for the feelings underneath the longing and started to honor them in movement (which is the heart of PON), she ultimately decided she did not care about the extra twenty pounds and did in fact go on to find a deeply loving, respectful, and responsible partner.

Kathy was right. There was trauma stored in those 'extra' twenty pounds, but it was the trauma of unexpressed anger – not the weight itself.

Look, we all know what it is to want something but not know how to get it. We all know what it is to want to change something in our lives, or in our relationships, and feel lost about how to do that.

What is interesting and exciting is when you discover that the very thing that is causing you to question is the very thing that has the answer.

In other words, what you want to change is the very thing that will help you change it. Whaaaa? Hang with me here.

TOUCH CAN BE TERRIFYING

I met Melanie in jail where she awaited trial for drug possession. She came to my movement class because she wanted to get out of her cell and away from her "bunkie" (roommate).

Our first class, I taught a pose on our stomachs on the floor in order to stretch out our shoulders and necks.

I tried for a whole two minutes to explain how to do it. For some reason, Melanie just couldn't understand my instruction. (Now, I am more than willing to take responsibility for giving crappy directions, but everyone else figured it out after just a few prompts.) I even tried getting on my own stomach to demonstrate, but somehow, she just couldn't figure it out, though I could see she really tried.

There is a rule in jail that no one may give or receive touch. The rule was softer for those of us who came in from the "outside," and I had on occasion offered a slight finger or hand for direction.

Well, after those two minutes – and a great deal of laughter amongst the group – I asked Melanie if it would be alright if I touched her shoulders to show her how to do it. She paused and got still.

"I haven't been touched in eighteen months," she said.

"Would it be alright if I do so now?" I asked.

She cried, and said softly, "Yes, that sounds alright."

I placed my hand under her right shoulder girdle and shifted it over so she could lie down and roll over to stretch it.

The whole group – all eleven of the other ladies who were awaiting trial and away from their families – got quiet, as if watching something important.

As Melanie stretched her shoulder, I stayed next to her – not touching, just paying attention.

She stayed quiet – much calmer now and seemingly able to focus.

As she sat up, she said, "I was freaked out on the floor. I didn't know what was behind me. It felt like when I had to sleep at my uncle's house, and he was crazy." "Not a safe place to be," I offered.

"Oh hell, no," she answered.

The whole group seemed to exhale, and we then spent the rest of the class in an extraordinary conversation about safety, the lack of it, and how we reacted to danger.

These women – imprisoned, many guilty of crimes, almost all survivors of violence themselves – were able to share with each other the ways they shut down, drank, or drugged as a way to feel safer.

And all because of a shift a single touch caused.

One intervention with her body and Melanie tapped into an entire new way of being.

This book is not about sex per se or any particular way you move or feel.

It is a book about your body.

It is a book about ending your belief that you are inadequate and finally discovering you are not just enough – but all you desire.

It is a book about meeting yourself where you are and discovering you are already magnificent.

THE UNIQUE YOU

This book is a global practice for anyone with a body.

And everybody is unique. Your body – and your experience of it – is entirely your own. As no one ever before has had your exact face, fingers and toes, so too no one has had your exact experiences.

I want to acknowledge that some are happily asexual and enjoy intimacy in nontraditional ways.

Furthermore, we are all genders and all along the sexual continuum. We may love people of one sex and become intimate with another one. We may identify as one thing, and we may identify as many.

At the most core level, however, we are all human. We all have bodies, and as such, we all have our own gloriously unique, human experiences. It is to those experiences that this book is dedicated.

In this book, I write using "you," "he," and "she" mostly from the perspective of the clients I serve, but I invite you to come along, and please feel free to insert your own pronoun, identity, and any other qualifier which helps make you more able to take ownership of the stories, the insights, and the practice.

In any case, you, he, she, or they, we all want freedom, love, and peace.

One other side note:

There is good news and some hard news too.

Hard news first – you may find that there is a valid and important reason you are uncomfortable in your body. It may be that some of the ways you are living your life right now are not in alignment with your most loving self. It may be that you are being touched in a way that does not work for you. It may be that at one time you were touched in a way that was bad for you and your body remembers.

It may be that by going through the steps of this book you remember something that has been buried or has tried to stay hidden. But guess what? It's not hidden. It is actively affecting and informing your life right now. By allowing it to stay out of your awareness

– and your care – it will go right on affecting you and making you suffer.

Ready for the good news? The good news is that by addressing the challenges above and learning how to be in touch with your highly intelligent body, you will find renewed energy and joy. By learning to connect to your body in a positive way, your perspective on everything – not just the challenging things but the little ones – feels easier, brighter, more optimistic.

What was a place of suffering becomes the place of the greatest pleasure.

CHAPTER 2

IT FEELS LIKE DYING

When I was three years old, my father, who was drunk at the time, came into my room and assaulted me.

He was unable to penetrate my body, but to this day I know precisely where in my body he pushed against young flesh.

I am pretty sure it was the only time he tried to do that, but once was enough.

I successfully repressed the memory until I was almost thirty years old.

The truth of that trauma never went away, and it shaped my entire being.

From the ages of three to six, my father continued to drink, and my mother fell deeper into her own mental illness. I am told that before I was born, she heard the voice of God on the radio. Apparently, her own PTSD with psychotic features included a belief that she was the Virgin Mary. She, too, was an incest survivor.

By the time I was six, the marriage had come apart, and my parents announced their divorce. They told us solemnly and with an air of great drama. My sister and

I sat tucked together on the sofa in the living room. I believe I laughed.

And then, life changed quite dramatically. My father found a new girlfriend, and his career took off. He became happier, more stable – even healthy. He introduced us to protein shakes and took us to the ballet and on long walks which ended at the zoo. He even eventually stopped drinking.

My mother worked hard to get well too. Her greatest recovery was when she chose to identify as an alcoholic and compulsive overeater and found great support and healing in the twelve-step programs.

She never gave up trying to grow and be the best person she could be. She continued fighting for her own recovery until she passed away from breast cancer at sixty-one years old.

And so, somehow, the years of my young childhood became as if they never existed.

It was as if since my parents were different, my own experience was no more. There was no connection to the way they – and my life – had been.

I completely repressed the memories until after I left the house, graduated from a master's program, established a career in mental health, and married happily.

It wasn't until I was thirty years old that the memories came rushing back while doing my own therapy. The healing was hard and pushed me to places I had never been, but I finally got to where I felt I had my own life on my own terms.

It took me twelve years.

But the early experience never really went away.

What happened to me – even when forgotten – informed the person I became.

One consequence of the abuse was a deep and swift disassociation from my body.

When a child is hurt in the way I was, she learns that the world is unsafe; that feeling of unsafety is unsustainable over a lifetime - too much despair - so, she adjusts. With the extraordinary resilience of the Spirit, the child learns to compensate, and crafts ways to make it feel safe. She creates a worldview that makes what has happened logical and tolerable.

As a child, I discovered my body was an unsafe place to be, so I left it.

Further, I discovered the world made sense when I realized that I must be here to exist for other people. If I was here to be fully myself, it made no sense that those who were supposed to support me would use me in the ways they did.

So the "I" of me left my body, and the "I" that remained worked to function in the way that made sense: to be for other people.

This meant, of course, that I could never be quite sure what the best thing for me was.

Not really sure what I liked or where I wanted to go. I knew I wanted to feel safe and loved. But beyond that, I knew how to listen and try to get those things I craved (safety! love!).

I existed like that for a long time.

And then.

My youngest child went to kindergarten. Before he went, I had thoroughly enjoyed taking time away from my professional career to be a full-time mom. I loved being with my kids.

But then? The house was my own. For the first time in my life, I had substantial time to be with myself. I wasn't navigating childhood, or school, or career, or a relationship. I didn't need to use my energy to survive, learn, develop, or grow. I simply *was*. It freaked me out a little. I think I watched a lot of *The Dog Whisperer.*

I planned to go back to work but wasn't sure exactly what it would be.

Before pausing to be a full-time mom, I had enjoyed a long and varied career in clinical social work.

Working with women and violence was my earliest training and experience. In graduate school I worked at a sexual assault survivors' clinic in Chicago, where I loved helping empower women on their healing journeys.

Before graduate school, I did a yearlong training in psychodrama and group therapy, working with populations as diverse as the chronically mentally ill, forensic, and drug addicted. I used those skills when I briefly went into health education, where I had my first direct encounter with the intersection of mind and body, leading hospital workshops on stress management and assertiveness training.

After that, I became a social worker at a community health center for children and families. My caseload was filled with families in crises and in need of the most basic care.

Even then, I knew talking alone wasn't quite enough. Even when I worked with families in extreme situations – state-mandated treatment, poverty, abuse – I still wanted to know if they had been able to get a good night's sleep or breathed some fresh air. It was clear to me even then that total wellness could not be found if the body wasn't included in the treatment.

I knew that when I went back to work it was going to have to be something which addressed the physical body, as well as the emotional one.

So when my youngest went to kindergarten, I decided it was time for me to go back to school too, and I started a second masters in "body centered psychotherapy."

I never completed the program because my wise professor took one look at me one day and said, "Oh save the tuition. Just put your dang shingle up and start." So I did.

COMING BACK TO LIFE

While figuring out what to do professionally when my kids went back to school, I decided to have some fun too, and joined the local theatre troupe. My first production was *Cabaret*. I'm not sure my character had a name, but I got to sashay and sway, and (literally) kick up my heels.

I had so much fun, I joined a dance group and went every week to stomp, sweat, roll, press, and generally have a great time. And connect to my Body.

About a year into dancing, I woke up one morning and thought, "Oh my God. This is my body. This is my life!"

The dancing made everything feel totally new and yet somehow completely familiar.

It felt like I had landed for the first time on the planet I already inhabited. I felt more energized and in a better mood than usual. I was more patient with my kids and nicer to my husband. I somehow didn't mind that I still carried the extra baby weight or that I had circles under my eyes from being up at night.

When I danced, it was as if the me whom I repressed – or had been cauterized by the trauma – came back online. Suddenly, I knew what clothes I wanted to wear and what foods I wanted to eat. I knew what my opinions about things were and what I thought about this and that.

Oh, it didn't happen all over night. It took me years to figure some of that out. I am still figuring it out. But something happened in that movement – extra weight and all. It wasn't just the clothes and food and opinions, it was *me*. The I who I repressed came roaring back, and she had some things to say. I found out that I wasn't expressing my physical body in the way it craved. I found out that many of the choices I made about how I lived my life were not what my body wanted. I am afraid I even found out that the marriage I was in (and the beautiful man to whom I was married) was somehow an expression of a self I no longer was, and several years later, we divorced. (Miraculously, it was a tender and respectful divorce in which we were able to maintain the best of what we had been together and as a family.) When the true self is online, (so too is love.)

It was a time of endings and beginnings. It was a time of exhilaration and disruption. It was a time to become me and to find out I was there all along. The I who I thought I had abandoned and left behind? I found it exists always and cannot be destroyed.

It poked me and whispered in my head, "This is uncomfortable." "I am not dumb." "I want to stretch." "I want to feel alive." "I want to come back to, and live in, my body."

Oh, it took twenty years of being away from the danger in childhood, and making life as safe as it could be, so I didn't have to protect myself from that which made me leave my body in the first place.

All the ways I had been living out of fear – in particular, the belief I should 'be for everyone else' so I could anticipate what they needed and give it to them in order to make sure they could not hurt me" – became instead the whispers of discomfort and dissatisfaction and made me realize I could no longer sustain the dissociated, bargain-sale of my soul.

I wanted to know – and be – me for once.

And perhaps most exciting, I got clear about what I wanted to do with my career, and connected for the first time with clarity to what felt like my soul's purpose.

I brought together my background in psychotherapy, training in somatics and expressive therapies, and opened the doors to my first series, "Dancing to my Self."

This became my business for several years. I traveled around North America with a talented musician doing workshops on drumming and dancing. And while traveling, I continued to spend many hours refining the language for our workshops, ever eager to convey the message of the life-changing possibilities of awakening the self in motion.

In my search for language, I found the glorious world of yoga.

I discovered that yoga – particularly Kripalu yoga – had already crafted not only the language but an entire architecture to explore the power of personal exploration.

I did my first 200-hour teacher training there, and it will always be a place to which I return, as a way to connect to the value of compassionate self-witness.

But after a while, as I had previously felt in my psychotherapy practice a resistance to only talk, in the yoga I found a longing to explore the content of what the movement was stirring. Further, I discovered that Vedic yoga actually seeks to detach from the body rather than embrace it. Tantra yoga (which I discuss more in Chapter 5) helped remedy this, but even it did not have space for the full range of my modern, psychotherapeutically trained, feminist, trauma-surviving Self.

I recognized that ultimately all of the extraordinary teachings I had been exposed to and all of the life experiences I had were all just different ways to learn best about how to be in the moment I am in. And it is in the body I experience the moment.

The next step was to bring it all together: the social work degree, the clinical, psychodrama and group therapy training, the ecstatic dance, the yoga, the personal experiences, and mostly, all the exceptional men and women with whom I have had the gift of working, dancing, and exploring – and developed the Practice of Now.

This is a story about how the deep knowing of the body found its way back to itself.

This is a story about how connecting to the body connects you to your deepest, most true self.

This is a story about how that true self may lead you into and through challenges but also how it does so because it is leading you to the greatest and happiest expression of you.

It is a story about how the true self knows how to find its way to joy.

It is a story about how dance can save your soul.

It is my story. It is your story.

It is now.

CHAPTER 3

THERE IS A WAY!

Your body is a wonderland.

Right now, it feels like enemy territory or perhaps like nothing at all.

You relate to it as a place to avoid, overcome, or fight against.

But the fact is that your body is an exceptional network of information that is working twenty-four hours a day, seven days a week to keep you well.

In this chapter, you will learn about the Practice of Now (PON), and how engaging with it will free you from the fight within and bring you not just into peace but into joy. Your body is a highly intelligent and loving system that wants nothing more than for you to be – and feel – healthy, vital, and whole, and PON is going to take you and re-mind you. PON is going to re-connect you to that extraordinary system.

The Practice of Now insists that at this very moment – this very moment as you sit reading these very words! – freedom and joy are your birthright – and in fact, who you are – *because* you have a body.

And, in this chapter, you will learn the overview of the process you are about to undertake, and learn to orient to your body in an entirely new way.

Ready?

Here we go!

THE BODY IS THE WAY

Betsy came to one of my movement workshops because her friend brought her. She didn't really want to come because she heard there was going to be "dance," and she knew she definitely wasn't a dancer. In fact, she really didn't like to move much at all. She was fifty-two years old, had some knee issues, and always felt silly at parties or clubs when other people tried to drag her onto the dance floor.

After our introductions, she shared that her father had died ten months before, but she didn't really have much time to grieve the loss, as her business demanded her attention and her second child was still in the house. She suspected her father's death was having an impact at home because since then she had lost interest in her husband and preferred to go out with friends (even to this weird thing!) than stay at home with him.

When we arranged ourselves around the room to begin, she chose the furthest spot from the front, tucked into a back corner.

We all had instructions to keep our eyes gently closed or, if open, to keep our gaze soft, within our own spaces.

Lying down on the ground, the steady drum beat of the music began. Little by little, students were invited to notice just what was happening in our physical bodies. Tight shoulders? Rumbling belly? Achy knee?

Without needing to fix a thing, we then gently explored moving our bodies – piece by piece – in whatever way felt natural or available. We simply listened to the music, and without planning or arranging or watching, we just asked first the feet, "How do you feel like moving? Wanna stretch or roll? Stand or stamp?"

At first, Betsy was hesitant, but with time and the recognition that no one was watching, as well as a bit of the "what the heck" feeling, she started to move her own way.

By the time we made our way up into the spine and skull, she was in it. She remembered what it was like when she was a kid and danced around the living room, alternating between being a ballet dancer and an Olympic diver. She remembered what it was like to move without constraint or judgment.

And then I instructed the group to pause.

Without judgment but with curiosity, I invited the exploration of the ways we weren't moving. Was there a direction a dancer hadn't picked? An angle she avoided? How about speed or force? With gentleness, participants were invited to introduce the unfamiliar, different movements to the body to test it out. Sometimes there was just a big, clear, "No," and so it was let go. Sometimes there was humor or a feeling of awkwardness, but it felt okay to explore, and so the dancers did.

Little by little, we got curious about the places of "yes" in our body, and the "no's." Without thinking much about it, we opened to the question of the ways that the no's might be our own or perhaps might be others' – either taught to us or imposed.

Building heat in the body by moving rigorously for just six minutes, we built an alchemical fire. By raising the temperature in our own bodies, we tapped into the transformational power of fire and let that fire burn. Without thinking much about it but asking the body to guide us, we opened to the possible release of some of the no's that weren't our own.

For some of us it was clear what we were releasing: a belief we were too fat or too old; a fear we had to stay small to be loved, or to keep smiling when we really wanted to scream.

For some of us, we simply knew we were releasing the abstract no's that no longer served us and which were ready to be let go.

Betsy reported not thinking too much but having a general sense that she was really pissed and tired of playing small in her life and with herself.

After building that fire, what needed to be released was offered up in order to be taken away. Some cried; some yelled. Some simply threw their arms hard, as if pushing away the years of the debris and bullshit.

Betsy felt a blinding, white light pitch through her spine, down into her feet, and a kind of opening at the top of her head.

As the music got quieter, there was a general panting and feeling of relief in the room.

Betsy, meanwhile, remembered being a little girl and going for a bike ride with her dad, who taught her how to ride. She remembered falling off and him scolding her for her carelessness. (Interestingly, she fell on the same knee that bothers her to this day.) At the time, she felt a deep shame and a profound sense of not being adequate for her highachieving, athletic father.

As she lay there on the floor, with access to how she felt – now both in her body and in her heart – she realized that the feeling of being inadequate was still how she felt to this day. And she didn't want to feel it anymore. She recognized the feeling of inadequacy had played a role in her marriage and had affected her ability to be fully present with her husband – and in their sex life. She had stayed with her own body as it was, danced with it, opened to an exploration of it, and found it had lessons to teach and options to explore.

Now this was just one experience of one woman, but it demonstrates how by making space for the exploration of your body – and your feeling state – you open to the truth of the moment, which then gives you access to information about where you want to go next. This is what the Practice of Now will do for you.

THE PRACTICE OF NOW

In order to make your way back to love, you need to first find ways to get comfortable actually being in the moment. For some of us, that by itself is an enormous task.

Sometimes actually hanging out with what is going on inside of us is kind of a big no.

In fact, to avoid the no, you may have refined the art of deflection or disassociation. You shop. You eat. You drink. You daydream. You can probably find a hundred ways to avoid what is actually in the now, rather than to experience the depth and range of what you are feeling.

Here, we welcome feeling as our teacher. This does not mean that you let the feelings make your decisions for you. Rather, you cultivate an awareness of them as a kind of road map to your highest intelligence.

This intelligence is your soul, your highest self, the force that wants the best and most joy for you.

The Practice of Now is the pause of the outside world in order to cultivate personal time and space and then hear that wisdom roaring to come out.

When Tina came to me, she was fifteen pounds under her medically suggested weight. Otherwise healthy, she did not identify herself as having an eating disorder but knew eating was an issue keeping her from how she wanted to feel.

In one of our very first sessions, she shared that as a child, her father had been a heroin addict and her mother a highly anxious enabler. Her mother made clear that in order for her to be calm enough to parent Tina, she needed Tina to be quiet, pretty, and clean. As early as four, Tina remembered living in terror she would disrupt the brief, fragile moments of peace when they finally arrived. In particular, she remembered needing to make sure her room was spotless and would even sit on the floor in order not to mess anything.

In PON, Tina made room to reconnect to that part of her which still felt like she had to sit on the floor and be still. She could feel the ways that part wanted her to be not just still but small and as little as possible. In fact, shrinking was soothing. The idea of being big was terrifying.

By connecting to this in her feeling body, she could identify how it wanted to express itself (small, still). And the small, still part did not want to move.

At this juncture in the practice, Tina could make a conscious choice to stay in that somatic truth – a perfectly legitimate choice – or she could begin to lovingly introduce different ways of being. In her case, simply walking around the room while feeling vulnerable was transformational.

With time, Tina was able to become more comfortable with the sensations in her body as the gateway to the moment and, by doing so, to take ownership of the moment she wanted to craft.

The Practice of Now does no more than connect you to the Truth you already are. Childhood, family systems, life experiences, and your own subsequent sustaining world views keep you separate from that Truth.

PON will peel away the layers that separate you from that wisdom and, by doing so, connect you to your most blissful state.

Dina was a tall, thirty-six-year-old woman who came to my office because she recently became anxious during sex. She ruled out medical issues; her body was healthy and strong, but sex was unpleasant. She was involved with a man whose company she enjoyed but who "didn't turn her on" – which was kind of okay because she didn't want to have sex anyway.

After a few sessions – and committing to the Practice, she noticed a persistent pain in her lower left abdomen – a kind of sharp, radiating throb that would come and go during the day. With some patient and gentle exploration, she identified the pain with how she felt about being a tall, thin woman of color. She felt self-conscious about both and recognized that feeling so "seen" made her feel that she was being judged and found inadequate. She remembered being a child and being made fun of when she was the tallest one in class.

Dina was able to put together that her new boyfriend – who was not much shorter, but enough to be a trigger – was stimulating old feelings of inadequacy and judgment. Her feeling of inadequacy and fear had completely cut her off from being able to receive any positive touch from him. Even when he was thoughtful and trying hard to please her, she could not accept it because she felt unworthy.

With time and a direct interaction with that old wound, Dina identified the source of her resistance to sex and worked with her boyfriend to create a safe, comfortable environment in which she could release old hurts and open to his (non-judgmental and totally turned on) affection.

By taking time to listen to her body and refine her attention to what she felt, she found a road map to the answers she needed to create the situation she desired.

You may find some truths that want to hide. You may find there are reasons you haven't wanted to be touched or have felt disconnected to or uncomfortable with your body.

It is crucial you know that you are totally in charge of this process.

Too many of us have been told in too many ways how to accommodate, defer, and compromise.

This is your practice. It is not mine. It is not your husband's. It is yours.

In fact, the very heart of this practice is for you to connect to you. Whatever. However. Wherever. The best of you is already inside. The most alive, sensual, fierce goddess is waiting to come out. I promise. This is who you are.

We are going to find the ways in which she has been kept down and kept back. It is time to free Her – and You. It will happen in seven steps:

STEP ONE: YOU FIRST

To be comfortable with your body, you have to be comfortable being you. Knowing your own body is also the first step to get clear about what you want to heal and how you want to be.

STEP TWO: YOUR BIOLOGY

To be comfortable in your own skin, you need to know – and not judge! – your body. Our biology is an intelligent system and offers important information to understand what you need in order to enjoy touch.

Your body and biology are who you are – and who you are is perfect.

STEP THREE: YOUR HEART

After you are connected to your biology, you will have to be connected to your feeling. We often confuse "being" feeling with actually "feeling." Feeling is both in the body and in the heart, and you have to learn how to connect to both.

STEP FOUR: YOUR BODY

Learn practical skills how to be in and feel the body and heart as a way to feel vital and creative. Learn movement analysis and principles of yoga as tools to tolerate, sustain, and welcome sensation.

STEP FIVE: START TO MOVE

When you move authentically, you deepen your ability to stay present and feel pleasure. The power of personal movement clarifies and connects you to your natural instincts, and your natural instincts know how and when you want to be touched and to be. Remember, this can be in stillness.

STEP SIX: FREE THE BLOCKS

Find and release the parts of you that keep you uncomfortable with and outside of your body. By releasing the blocks, you will be able to enjoy sensations in your body more.

STEP SEVEN: LET LOVE MOVE YOU

Learn how to practice spontaneous and genuine movement as an expression of yourself. Dancing your own
way is a method of expressing yourself honestly, personally, powerfully, and joyfully. When you dance, you
connect to that part of you that is fully yourself and
knows if – and how – you want to be touched. By being
fully yourself, you are open to true intimacy – because
you are being intimate with yourself in the most genuine and profound way.

A few notes before you begin:

This first time, go through the steps one by one and
in order. You may want to skip ahead and do just one
or another. Eventually, that is more than okay! One
step may be all you need to get you back home. But
this first time, please at least read them in order.

This is because this ultimately is a somatic (i.e. physical) practice. And your mind will want to adjudicate,
evaluate, and control. It will want to tell you which step
works better, and which step you don't need.

Bless the mind! It keeps you safe and functioning.
But here (ironically?), you want to let it be dismantled
piece by piece. In the Practice of Now, there will be
time and space for interpretation and evaluation. But
first? Learn how to listen to and awaken your connection to your body.

By following through the steps in order, you will make your way from the shallow end of the pool to the deep end. Only when you have made your way deliberately and with compassion can you lift your feet off the floor and swim.

CHAPTER 4

YOU FIRST

"The roar of joy that set the whole world in motion
is reverberating in your body
And the space between all bodies.
Beloved, listen. Listen.
Find the exuberant vibration
Rising new in every moment,
Humming in your secret places,
Resounding through the channels of delight.
Know you are flooded by it always.
Float with the sound.
Melt with it into divine silence.
The sacred power of space will carry you Into the dancing
radiant emptiness That is the source of all.
The ocean of sound is inviting you
Into its spacious embrace,
Calling you home"
– Radiance Sutras, v 16 – Translated by Lorin Roche

This chapter is designed to reconnect you to you. You need to know how and who you are in order to establish a positive relationship with your body. Like any good relationship, you and your body need to actually know each other before you can be close.

In fact, feeling close will be the result of knowing each other better. And feeling close naturally leads to compassion. It's a lot easier to demonize a stranger than it is a friend But why?

Because your body may be a battleground, but it is also the site of your greatest dreams.

The very place you want to avoid or fix is also the very place you want to feel better. Your experience of your body is both how you are suffering and how you will know you are not.

This means your entire journey is within – and in the experience of – your body. You and your relationship with – you.

SO WADDYA THINK?

"Watch your thoughts, they become words;
watch your words, they become actions; watch your actions,
they become habits; watch your habits, they become charac-
ter; watch your character, for it becomes your destiny."
– Frank Outlaw, Late President of the Bi-Lo Stores

A 2009 study conducted by The Telegraph asked one hundred women to carry a clicker to measure how many times they felt anxiety about their bodies. Over a seven-day period, women aged thirty-five to sixty-nine had to use the clicker every time they worried about their face, body, or appearance in general. On average, the women surveyed had negative thoughts thirty-six times a day. That's more than two negative thoughts for every waking hour.

In the 2016 *Glamour* survey, ninety-six percent of women reported having severe negative thoughts about their body throughout the course of a day. On average, the participants had thirteen (highly) negative body thoughts per day or one negative thought for every hour awake.

Right now, you don't like the way you feel or look. When you step out of the shower, or bath, and see yourself in the mirror, you recoil. You have stories about how you are supposed to be and the ways you believe you fall short. You think you are too old, too fat, too thin. You think you need to take some part away or add something on. Simply put, you think you are either too much or not enough.

The trick is for every thought you have, you define how you feel. Not only is the thought itself painful, but when you produce it, your body hears and responds accordingly.

Remember Linda, from Chapter One? She could not walk by a mirror without looking directly at her stomach and thinking, "Ugh. So fat." She would inevitably start to worry about what she was going to eat (or not) and eventually actually start to feel bloated. Her bloating became so much of an issue she sought medical help, but the doctors told her there was nothing wrong with her digestive system. It was her *thoughts* that were creating her experience of herself and her experience of her body.

You have become so used to judging, analyzing, and then avoiding your body, you forget how to actually relate to it.

Like any relationship, you need to be in connection and in dialogue in order to converse about what each of you needs and how to move forward.

And like any relationship or pen pal, the more you reach out, the more your body will reach back.

It is time to acquaint yourself with you.

TAKING INVENTORY

MIRROR EXERCISE

It is time to take stock not just of how your body and feelings are but also how your thoughts are influencing what you feel.

This one is going to feel hard but will be crucial to undoing the patterns which have kept you battling with your body.

You need to be able to witness and know what is racing around in there. You need to truly know the state of things as they are.

Find time to be alone and private.

Bring a journal with you.

If you can stand it, take your clothes off and do this naked. For some of us, that is too much, too soon. But if it is available, you may be astounded by the quality of what your thoughts tell your body. You may be shocked or perhaps all too acquainted with the savagery of your commentary.

If clothes off is too much, start with just your face.

You may find that looking at yourself triggers a stream of responses. You may find that it's almost impossible to hear even one specific thought and all you are aware of is a rash of feeling.

This is all right. Stay with this. Make some space to simply allow the "what is." This is not an exercise in improvement. This is not an opportunity to beat yourself up one more time. There is nothing to fix, dear heart. Remember, all you need to do is pay attention and be compassionately curious.

Know that you are not any one thought. This is simply what is moving in and through you at this one moment.

We are going to dance with it all later.

WALKING OUT EXERCISE

This exercise can be done independently or in tandem with the above exercises.

The purpose of this exercise is to begin to track how your inside relationship with your body affects what you do with it on the outside.

This simply entails bringing the same inquiry of the Mirror exercise to how you dress.

What clothes do you wear?

What mask/role do you wear over that body when you interact with the world?

For three days, journal what you wear and your thought process when you chose your outfit. Be specific. Notice if you put something away because it is too revealing or too tight or torn. Notice how you are feeling about your body when you make those choices.

This might feel burdensome or laborious. But consider it like one of those food programs where you try to figure out if you have allergies. You have to take stock of what you are putting in (on!) your body before you know what to take out (off)! That is all.

JOURNAL EXERCISE

During this exercise, you may write just once or as often as you like. The first time, sit down with no distractions and imagine you are visiting with your best friend in the whole world whom you haven't seen in a year. She and you tell each other everything. This time, your body is your best friend, and you want to know everything she has to share. Everything!

Sometimes your friend will just give you those bullet points of news: This happened, then that. I went there, then here. Your entry will be direct and straight forward, like one of the first ones I wrote when I began my own body healing journey.

Journal Entry, August 2006

Belly full. Bloated. Kinda sweaty after my shower. My feet hurt too.

When I pause like this, I can feel my heart beat. Kinda weird, kinda scary.

Sometimes the entry may be deeper and describe something beyond the obvious physical body.

The more you practice paying attention – without judgment, compromise or evaluation – the more you will be able to explore the feelings under the feelings.

After one particularly painful flare up of my back injury, I wrote this:

Journal Entry, October 2007

My back hurts.

The pain begins in my L5 and radiates throughout my low back. I can feel it in my jaw and in the grip of my teeth and then across my chest and heart and down to my neck.

There is such a tightness. A deep pain. I can feel it like a contraction, a pulling in. It wants to hold on and never let go. It wants to keep me in its grip so I cannot be free, never be loose. It is pulling, tugging insistently down and down into itself. DO NOT MOVE, it says. Stay absolutely still. You may not. Shall not. And so, it becomes the Cannot.

Good, it says. Stay bound. You belong to me. Shutter the lights. Close the blinds. Do not look. Do not peek. STAY STILL. FREEZE.

And then, the Voice. The longing. The rage. The fighting back. The wish to be soft and let go. It is all here.

I WANT TO BE FREE OF THIS SUFFERING. I WANT TO BE FREE OF THE CONTRACTION.

There is no wrong way to do this exercise. This is simply a way to begin to dial up the volume of what already is happening.

There is only you and you. Like the best kind of friendship, how and the way you communicate will be strictly your own.

The only rule is that you care. Care, pay attention, and let her tell you whatever she wants to tell you.

ROMANCING THE BONES

It is time to get to know the true you and find out how spectacular you actually are.

Consider this:

At the most basic level, your body has an almost magical ability to heal. When you cut your finger, the skin will heal. If you break a bone, it will knit.

And please note that this is all without your thinking mind. If you had to do what the body does every second, you would certainly expire within seconds.

The body wants to be well. It is constantly working to stay healthy and, in fact, to seek out what does not serve its well-being.

Your white blood cells and entire antibody system are constantly at work to root out illness and keep you healthy.

This intelligence is your salvation and the way back into your own state of wellness.

Further, do you agree humans have evolved from a less-complex life form? Amoebas and apes? Do you believe that biological creatures are in a process of evolution? That you have progressed from those sea life anemones to Neanderthals, to humans. Agreed?

Well, if your biological matter has been doing that, why not whatever animates you – your biology - and what makes you unique? What about your spiritual self?

Could it not be possible that who you are as a human – all of it – is still evolving?

I call this your Spiritual Immune System.

Well, my love, if we can just get you to tap into that wisdom, you will need less and less of your (necessary but)super judgmental mind to get you out of whatever mess you are in.

Let's start by getting on the same page about the perfection of your body as it is.

Don't worry – we're going to spend quite a bit of time on this. This is just to get you started.

Emma was forty-six when I first met her at my yoga class for women in jail. She was tall, with a tattoo of a waffle on her arm and a deep, hoarse laugh from a lifetime of smoking.

She liked the stretching, and I could tell the yoga philosophy we often discussed in class intrigued her.

But it was during her fourth session, when I led students in a simple body scan to notice what they were feeling, that I saw her cry softly.

When we went around the room to check in, she lifted her head and said sadly, "I don't know what I feel."

I sat quietly for a moment, as the class digested what she said.

"I don't know that I ever really have. When I was little, my dad used to beat me pretty bad, and I would just checkout, y'know?"

Half of the class nodded, murmuring they knew what she meant.

Lee, who had been arrested on prostitution charges, spoke up and said, "It's better that way."

Emma blew her nose and offered, "No. That means my dad still owns me. I want to get myself back so I can know what I need. I don't want to wind up in jail again, and I am pretty sure to stay out I gotta figure out how to take care of myself."

Over the course of a few months, the women and I worked to see what it was to actually feel and pay attention to the personal body, and re-craft a new relationship with what had been a stranger.

One day, Emma bounded into class and said, "Oh my God! I actually did the thing, and just watched, and felt, and then the most amazing thing happened! Suddenly, all I could feel was love. It was crazy! I used to be terrified of my body, but now I actually feel like it can be my best friend!"

Sometimes when you consider taking time to put yourself first, you worry that this makes you selfish, and somehow may lead to hurting others with your selfishness.

Please know that this curiosity about you is not a selfish one. It is actually the first step in being able to love and receive love from another.

When you take the time to genuinely cultivate an interest in how you feel and who you are, you no longer need to go outside of yourself for the answers. You no longer need – or resent – the other who is not giving you what you need – because you know how to give it to yourself.

It is such a simple, sweet concept, and yet so many of us deny ourselves because we think it is more loving to do so. In fact, this practice says the opposite is true; when you do this work and pause long enough to tend to your own needs and vulnerabilities, you can face the blocks that keep you from becoming who you truly are.

And who you are is pure Love.

Knowing this is critical for your healing process:

You first.

You can't expect your partner – anyone for that matter – to know how to touch you or be with you in a way that feels good if you don't know what feeling good is.

You have to be comfortable in your own body before you can expect to be comfortable with someone else.

You have to learn how to be your own best friend. Let's figure out how to do that, okay?

LOVE LETTER EXERCISE

Take your journal, and put at the top, "Beloved, my love letter to you."

I want you to write the most audacious, over the top (but sincere) letter to yourself. Just start with the prompt, and write continuously for five minutes. Just five minutes without stopping.

I realize this will feel stilted, artificial, or even impossible.

So think of it this way: If you can't write it to you, just imagine what you want the most spectacular friend - or lover - to say to you in the quiet of your room. What words do you long to hear? What is the thing you most want to hear? Just riff on that.

We'll come back to this later.

LONGING FOR TOUCH

The thing is, we know we need skin touch. We know that the human body is designed to flourish when touched.

In the 1950's, Harry Harlow conducted research to determine just how important it was for us to have touch in our lives. At a time before ethical interventions of animal rights, Harlow conducted research with rhesus monkeys and their need for connection.

Harlow took infant monkeys from their biological mothers and gave them two inanimate surrogate mothers: one was a simple construction of wire and wood, and the second was covered in foam rubber and soft terrycloth. The first group of monkeys were allowed to pick between either the wire mother, who had a milk bottle and the cloth mother who did not. The second group of infants were allowed to pick either the cloth mother who had the food, or the wire mother who had none.

In both conditions, Harlow found that the infant monkeys spent significantly more time with the terrycloth mother than they did with the wire mother. When only the wire mother had food, the babies came to the wire mother to feed and immediately returned to cling to the cloth surrogates.

Those poor sweet things wanted above all else to feel physically comforted.

Recent research also shows that there is a science behind skin touch. Mothers and babies are biologically programmed to benefit from skin-to-skin contact. The newborn releases oxytocin, a chemical associated with calm and feelings of contentment– and so does the mother – when their skin touches. The oxytocin actually boosts the immune system and makes us less susceptible to illness.

It is a biological fact that when you developed as a human you were made in consort with another. Literally, your physiological development happened as an extension of another.

You were grown inside of another being, your mother, with whom you shared a biological (umbilical cord) connection.

And it is in your first breath that you experience your first separation. By becoming human/first being alive, you learn what it is to be apart and alone.

There then exists in us all a deep need to resolve that and, in some way, to return to that feeling of oneness.

Touch can be one way to feel connected. Literally.

For several months, I worked with a young woman who came to me because she was a dancer and deeply uncomfortable being touched in rehearsals and performances. She dreaded choreography that required her to touch other dancers. At the same time, she also felt increasing anxiety and isolation in other areas of her life.

After our third session, we worked on a body scan in which we went through the ordinary checking-in to physical sensations in the body.

Mia reported feeling "calm" on the top of her body, with maybe a little bit of tension in her left shoulder from exercising the night before. She felt very little in her torso and almost had no sensation in her pelvis or legs. But she noted when she got to her feet, she felt a bit of a sharpness in her right ankle.

We stayed with that. Just that. A bit of sharpness. I had her stand and slowly start to walk around the room. She reported little change in the sensation, but it was still sharp. I had her pause and start to create a more focused relationship with the feeling. What color was it? Did it have a sound? A shape? Maybe a little pink, with red lines. Kind of dark. Then I had her bend her knees and bring a little more weight onto her ankle. She stopped and said, "Oh ya. I am remembering I used to play soccer when I was in middle school, and I think I sprained my ankle like three times." After she breathed and I made sure she wasn't antagonizing an old injury, I had her resume her exploration.

She stopped again and, with eyes closed, said softly, "Oh my God. I just remembered I used to do cutting on my ankle."

She went on to remember that when she was in middle school, she started cutting behaviors (the systematic cutting of the skin as a way to discharge difficult emotion, and create a relationship with pain) on her ankle, thinking she could hide the scars under her socks.

And that was the beginning of a deeper inquiry into what was happening in her life at that time and how she had started a lifelong pattern of hating her body and feeling that the cutting both numbed and gave an outlet for that pain. She stopped the cutting by high school, but by then, she figured out how to stay permanently numb to her body.

During the Practice of Now, she began to understand that being touched for her forced her back into her body after a lifetime being able to stay outside of it. With the Practice, she slowly began to tolerate her own feelings and so could tolerate others feeling (!) her.

There were layers of work for Mia, but it began with the simple and direct inquiry of how her body was feeling.

CHAPTER 5

YOUR EXTRAORDINARY, ORDINARY BIOLOGY

Your body is a perfect organism and cosmos unto itself.

Nothing about you is a mistake. Every freckle, every challenge, every unique thing about you has a purpose and a reason for being.

In this chapter, you will learn how smart you are and how starting this Practice just as you are makes perfect sense.

THE INTELLIGENCE OF THE NERVOUS SYSTEM

Your body has a brilliant, built-in system perfectly designed to keep you alive and help you cope with life-threatening situations.

It may be that part of how you relate to your body is, in fact, a system at play which believes it is protecting itself from perceived danger. This does not mean that you are in danger. On the contrary, by becoming interested and exploring what is happening in your body, you can re-train your body to know that it is safe and feel more open to be vulnerable and accepting.

As you may recall from seventh grade science, you have two functioning nervous systems: First, the parasympathetic – sometimes called the "rest and digest" – system which helps keep the body in homeostasis, also known as your "resting state," by regulating your heart and digestion.

Your second is the "sympathetic" nervous system – sometimes referred to as the "fight or flight response" – which is where all sorts of interesting things happen.

The sympathetic nervous system helps your body to react to stress – and perceived threats – by making sure you stay alive. Primarily, it releases a chemical called corticosal steroid to assist the body to dilate the eyes, increase heart rate, constrict blood vessels, and shorten the breath cycle. It shortens the exhale mostly in order to hold the breath in. In a crisis, the body is not sure when it will be able to breathe again. Think about it. If a truck starts to barrel down the street at you, you gasp and hold your breath, right?

This is a high arousal state. The frontal cortex of the brain shuts down, and there is no access for "higher functioning" processing. Forget about having a thoughtful conversation; it's just "get me out of here and keep me alive." It can take twenty to sixty minutes for the cortex to return to its normal functioning state when there is an environment to support that.

When we experience a traumatic event – and this can be a perceived threat, rather than an actual threat to our physical lives – and cannot defend ourselves or are in a situation we cannot control with no ability to soothe the nervous system, we have no ability to return to normal. We are stuck in survival mode.

And no one feels beautiful or sexy when trying not to die.

Seriously. Who would ever expect someone recovering from trauma to be amorous? I am not saying this is you, but I am saying that there are logical, biological reasons the body might be wired or trained to resist certain stimuli.

Feeling shut down in this instance is not dysfunctional. It is, in fact, quite brilliant.

POLYVAGAL NERVE THEORY

A wonderful scientist by the name of Dr. Stephen Porges offers a perspective on human behavior which has direct bearing on your quest for touch and ease in the body.

It is called the Polyvagal Nerve Theory.

There is a portion of your brain called the limbic system which modulates emotions, memories and arousal/stimulation. Inside of it, there is a main nerve called the vagus nerve, which helps control muscles of the throat and plays a major role in regulating the heart rate and keeping the gastrointestinal tract in working order. The vagus nerves also carry sensory information from the internal organs back to the brain.

Porges' identifies this nerve as controlling your "social engagement" response. By this he means that in times of safety, it facilitates rest, relaxation, and digestion. However, in times of threat, it has a defensive mode.

When you feel threatened, you typically attempt to engage the resources of your social nervous system to re-establish a sense of connection and safety. If you are unable to create a safe, relational bond – because you are in a traumatic situation – you will resort to biobehavioral defense strategies, such as fight or flight to mobilize you into self-protection. Fight or flight response is the state of being ready to run or fight back. This may result in feelings of anxiety, shakiness, or panic.

Furthermore, says Porges, if your nervous system response is unsuccessful – and you still feel unsafe – you will default to the "dorsal vagal complex." This more primitive strategy engages the parasympathetic nervous system in defensive strategies such as dissociation or fainting. Here, you might feel tired, dizzy, or nauseous.

So if you have trauma in your background, you may be in a perpetual state of fight, flight, or freeze and have no way to discharge or change that sensation. As a result, you feel trapped or shut down constantly. You actually feel physically numb as a result of past fear.

So in a sense, there is an "evolutionary competence" to feeling immobilized.

Some people who survive trauma don't like being in social environments or with other people because it feels overstimulating. According to polyvagal theory, when the vagus nerve is in a state of stress, it is difficult to read and interpret facial expressions, as well as distinguish the human voice from background noise. Consequently, we get none of the reassurance we need from social interaction. Instead, a feeling of anxiety and separation develops.

We re-contextualize. Part of being traumatized can be a response to being angry at the body for somehow "not responding" the way we wished it to (fight or flee), when in fact, our bodies responded in just the way our survival apparatus was designed for it to respond.

It may be, then, that your body's experience of itself is actually a mode of survival. Your body may be engaged in highly logical, even lifesaving behaviors. When something about our environment triggers us, it may be an old response, but it is an appropriate response to an old memory.

The good news is you can learn to re-set your body's patterns.

ACE SCORE

One way to understand the state of your biology right now is to have a sense of where you have been. For some, specific somatic experiences in the past may very particularly impact how you feel in the present.

Childhood experiences, both positive and negative, help shape the experience of our biology. Negative experiences may collectively accrue and affect physiological development. These are collectively referred to as Adverse Childhood Experiences (ACEs) and were systematized by a CDC-Kaiser Permanente study in 1997.

There are ten types of childhood trauma measured in the ACE Study. Five are personal physical abuse, verbal abuse, sexual abuse, physical neglect, and emotional neglect. Five are related to other family members: a parent who's an alcoholic, a mother who's a victim of domestic violence, a family member in jail, a family member diagnosed with a mental illness, and the disappearance of a parent through divorce, death, or abandonment. Each type of trauma counts as one. A person who's been physically abused, with one alcoholic parent, and a mother who was beaten up, has an ACE score of three.

According to the research, the higher the score, the higher a person's risk of adverse health outcomes, including substance use disorders and addiction. High doses of adversity actually affect brain development, the immune system, and the processing of hormones.

Such physiological responses have a direct impact on the felt experience of the body.

In order to find your ACE score, go to the following website: https://acestoohigh.com/got-your-ace-score/.

Don't worry if you're thinking, "Huh? What does this have to do with me? And yah, I know I have trauma, but now what?"

I promise we'll get to the how in Chapters 6 to 10.

Right now, we are building the case for the intelligence of the current state of your body.

When you can let go of judgment against your bodies' responses and recognize that the experiences in your body are responses to nervous system cues – which may be from very old trauma – you can begin to stop fighting against it.

Meryl first came to me with chronic neck pain. She mentioned it almost parenthetically to her 'presenting problem' of stress and job dissatisfaction. However, when we began the Practice, she realized the tightness in her neck was closely linked to the stress of her job. But it did not end there. With compassionate curiosity, she explored the nature and experience of the pain and was able to connect it to physical sensations she had as a child when her mother would tell her how unsafe the world was.

By connecting the physical pain to her childhood experiences, Meryl was able to work through those memories and heal the needs of her childhood self. This, in turn, led her to feel brave enough to change her work situation.

Jane was a thirty-year-old software developer who came to me because of her aversion to touch. She felt lonely but could not tolerate the company of people without feeling anxious and unhappy. She felt perfectly content with the size and shape of her body, but she could not stand feeling that it betrayed her every time she tried to get close with someone.

In our initial intake, she shared that in her childhood, she was exposed to domestic violence, neighborhood violence, and addiction. On an ACE score, she rated quite high.

With somatic therapy, she learned how to stay present long enough with her body's experienced state of perpetual of fight or flight and instead introduce it to new ways to move – and so, be.

Like Jane, who learned to engage her body in a proactive manner, you too can learn to interact with possible physiological responses to possible trauma and re-organize the body into a state of ease and well-being.

Change the body, change the brain.

CHANGE THE BODY, CHANGE THE BRAIN

Another critical feature of your remarkable body and biology is your brain's neuroplasticity.

It's only been about fifty years, but we now know that the brain can actually change itself. In what is known as functional plasticity, the brain can move functions from a damaged area of the brain to other undamaged areas. Further, in what is known as structural plasticity, the brain can change its physical structure as a result of learning.

In other words, we now know that the adult brain is far from being rigid or unchangeable, and whatever has been your pattern of being – even within the grooves of your brain – can change!

Why is this important? It's critical that we know this as we make space and get interested in the functioning and features of you.

You must know that whatever you discover in this practice, nothing about you needs to be "fixed" – especially the biology which you will be working hard to connect with and honor.

However, in as much as you discover the logic of how you have been, it is critical you know that it is absolutely possible to change.

And there will be times that you need outside help. You may seek out professionals – medical, homeopathic, or somatic, but for now, I want you to learn about your body's wisdom.

To paraphrase Leslie Kaminoff, a world-renowned anatomy expert and yoga therapist, "Even the day you die, there is more going right in your body than wrong."

Think about that. What this means is that at every moment, there are thousands – even millions if you think about the intelligence of every cell – systems at play to maintain and keep you going. A thousand ways that your body is actively seeking out the nourishment you need to function and actively seeking out the waste for you to release.

Your body is an act of acceptance, growth, and compassion. And when you listen to, and honor that body, you will find magic.

ANG SANG WAHE GURU: THE BODY IS LOVE

"Ang Sang Wahe Guru"

Translation: The dynamic, loving energy of the infinite source of all is dancing within every cell of you.

"Ang" is "cell" or "limb."

"Sang" is "in every part," or "with every part."

"Wahe" is the indescribable living ecstasy of infinite being.

"Guru" is wisdom or the knowledge that transforms your mind, emotions, and essence. This means the divine Universe – God, Love – is in your body.

In fact, your body is Love.

Tantra is an ancient practice that says simply, life is sacred – and that you enjoy the highest blessing of existence simply by having a human life.

Can we just dispel right away modern western craziness about tantra as a sexual practice? Oh, it can absolutely impact your sexuality, but that is only because your sexuality is part of who you are.

Tantra is a practice for life.

Tantra says that your body is an altar. The ultimate altar is that which is (felt) inside.

Furthermore, the body is designed perfectly for you to ascend to the highest form of ecstasy.

And if you are not experiencing life as sacred, it's because you haven't entered that relationship with yourself.

According to tantra, this means that your body, right now, has all the tools it needs to feel pure joy.

Unless you have personally activated your own potential, you cannot have an impact on the world or on the greater consciousness of which you are part.

This is good news for those of us who want to contribute to the world around us but still feel like we have work to do on ourselves.

In fact, the only way you actually can contribute is through the work of personal growth, empowerment, and self-actualization.

This is also good news for you because it means you get to do this work for you first and know that by definition it is going to benefit your relationship with your loved ones.

The last bit of tantra philosophy I want to share with you is the view that liberation – freedom from suffering – finding bliss – is actually found by living in "sacred reality". In this way, we can view everything as sacred: skin and bones, and subtle energies. The forces of nature, colors, sounds. We use everything at our disposal – all of this to bring out the best of ourselves.

Our job in our humanity is to find the places where we are locked away from our true power/divinity, and then connect to our true potential. And the more we bring our (true) selves to the practice, the more we unlock those powers.

Somatic therapy is the practice of cultivating a relationship with your body so you can plug into it as your teacher, guide, and guru.

Caring about the body becomes the actual gateway to your liberation.

RITCHIE

Ritchie's story is about a man who discovered actual, life changing magic within his own body.

When Ritchie was eleven, he became a drug mule for his uncle and father in West Texas. His family, while large and close, was heavily involved in drug crimes.

By the time he was sixteen, he was stealing cars and dealing on his own. Arrested for the first time soon after, he began a twenty-year cycle of arrest, jail, probation, re-offending, which then repeated.

By the time he was thirty-two, he had been arrested and jailed seventeen times. It was the life he knew, and while harsh, he didn't know any other.

The seventeenth time he was arrested, Ritchie was sent to county jail to await trial.

While there, he wound up in a yoga class with Greg – a hippy dude in dreadlocks who spoke softly and talked about how to breathe.

At first, Ritchie only went to class because it was a way to get out of his cell. Those first two classes he was pretty skeptical and not particularly impressed.

Then, on the third class, Greg started to teach about a pose called "crow."

It required balancing on hands while crouched over the floor. Ritchie, who was pretty athletic, thought it looked interesting and gave it a try. He realized pretty quickly that while it required core strength, it also required a certain courage to surrender because it meant to do it you might fall over – and on your face.

As he started and then stopped, Greg came over and crouched down next to him. Quietly, Greg told Ritchie he was "right there" and would be sure he would not let him fall.

Something shifted inside of Ritchie. Somehow, being engaged in a purely physical practice and hearing the kindness in Greg's voice, he trusted. In a real way, it was perhaps the first time in his whole life he trusted.

There, on a cold and dirty linoleum floor, eighteenth arrest and trial scheduled, he was held – near the floor, by Greg, and by his own hands – and he surrendered.

He was hooked. He kept coming for the following seven weeks and found out he loved the philosophy and the opportunities to explore the philosophy in the physical poses. He loved the practice of breathing and quieting the mind.

Then, his trial came. The judge, a familiar judiciary, sick of seeing Ritchie (and utterly dismissing Ritchie's claim of his innocence in this particular charge), sentenced him to six months of solitary confinement.

In solitary confinement, you live in a cell that is, on average, eight by ten feet and are typically allowed out to exercise for one hour or less.

You are alone for all of it. To leave your cell, you are handcuffed. Perhaps most cuttingly, when you walk by guards, they turn their backs to you, hands clasped, as a form of the solitary sentence.

It is a cruel and harsh way to live, and Ritchie was assigned to it for six months. All alone. Stuck in a cell with nothing to keep him busy.

The first month came and then went. By the second month, he decided to create a daily routine, and added the yoga Greg taught him. What else was there to do? He practiced what he learned: one foot here, one hand there. Breathe in. Breathe out.

Another month went by.

By the second month, he became dependent on those moments of physical concentration and quiet reflection. Six months came and went.

No release.

A bit desperate, he asked his mother to get him yoga books – but he was denied because they were deemed "entertainment" and "not rehabilitative."

He practiced those seven poses day after day until he knew them intimately.

Another month went by. No release.

More imprisoned than he ever had been in his life – no company, no way to distract himself or learn anything new, he turned to the only companion he had. He allowed his own breath and his own body to teach him.

Six months turned into thirteen.

When Ritchie left that cell, after he had gone in knowing seven postures and one breathing exercise, he left knowing fifty-two different actual yoga poses taught for almost a hundred years and in thousands of studios. His body and his breath were his only teachers.

This an absolutely, exquisitely, true story.

Your body holds the answers. Your body is brilliant.

CHAPTER 6

(THE ART OF) FEELING

Are you satisfied your biology has intelligence? If you are still skeptical, I want you to put this book down and, with your mind, try to do what your body is doing in the same amount of time. Now pick the book back up. Can we agree your body is smart?

Now it is time to know that what is moving through your body is also intelligent. And what is moving through you is feeling.

Your feelings are the very language of your most intelligent self – your soul. Your feelings are the way you communicate with you.

There are two different kinds of feelings. The first is what you associate with physical sensation, "The fire feels hot." "My hamstring feels tight." But there is a second kind of feeling, what you know as "emotion." This emotion comes not from your hamstrings or your fingers but from your heart. Your heart is the center of who you are.

In the yoga tradition, there are spirals of energy called the chakras along the spine – which is considered the center of the body. And the center of the center is the heart. Three chakras below and three above. (More on this in Chapter 8, when you will learn about how to engage with the chakras.)

Isn't it magical that the heart is both a biological fact, as well as an energetic one? What is in your heart is emotion and you.

In this chapter, you will learn the art of connecting to your feeling and so will learn the art of connecting to your soul.

THE SOUL

What is the soul?

Well, can we agree you are unique? I mean, forget about 'special' (though I know you are) – but how about just: you are an individual who has never before been and never will be again. Can we agree on that?

Well, what is that thing? Is there something that animates you personally? I mean, the way you watched that sunset or held your child or tasted that food – that is somehow all you, right? There is something that makes you who you are.

If you would like to describe that thing as strictly DNA or "science," okay. But there is something that makes you unique and has its own operating system, yes?

How do you know if you enjoyed that sunset? How do you know whether you liked that dish? How do you understand your response to your child, or your partner? Because of how you feel.

Take this one step further. How do you know what is best for you? How do you discriminate the myriad of options about what to do or not do and know what is most right and true for you? How can you know your soul's longing? How can you know soul's direction? Because of how you feel.

Not the feeling which is actually an opinion: "I hate that dress because it makes me look fat." "I love him because he has a good job." "I feel happy because the popular girl told me she likes me."

Not the feeling which is actually a thought. "I feel ugly because I have a fat stomach." "I hate myself because I made a mistake." This is the feeling that comes from your gut, your heart, your being.

Your mind is full of thoughts based on stories about who you have been and are supposed to be. Now I realize this may sound a bit weird or selfish somehow (review Chapter 1, please, on how focusing on the self is not selfish), but consider that the uniqueness of you both comes from, and is, your feeling. Does your soul have a phone to communicate what it wants you to know? No. It communicates through sensation.

Your soul speaks through your gut, your feet, your fingers, and your heart. Right? Who you are is what you feel. You feel; therefore, you are.

Of course you need the mind to help you make choices about how to act and react (more on this later), but feelings are dynamic, and what may be true for you one day will not be true the next. What your soul tells you is right for you today has room to shift and change.

You use the mind to discriminate out and make sense of it all, but the information is in the feeling.

How you feel inside of you. There is an art in this – and we will learn it together.

WHAT IS FEELING?

Dear one, in order to heal your intolerance and aversion to your own body, you have to know better what is underneath the aversion. The good news is that exploration also becomes the gateway through which you pass to find your way back to the love that you already are.

Your aversion – yes, even your 'neuroses' – come from your humanity. It is the crack through which you let the light in.

Light is merely that which illuminates dark. It shows us what is in the shadows; it does not make this thing go away. Its superpower is illumination.

Where you feel afraid, you learn how to be brave. Where you feel sad, you learn what is important not to lose. Where you feel joy, you learn what you want to keep or how you want to be.

You are the transformation.

And the transformation begins with you connecting with your feeling.

People often confuse 'being feeling' with actually feeling. Feeling is both in the body and in the heart, and in order to be free of your suffering, you need to learn how to connect to both.

THE BODY DOES NOT LIE

When I was thirty years old, I told my father I no longer wanted contact with him.

I needed to separate for my well-being and focus on my wonderful, new family.

It was a good decision, which made space for lots of personal growth and happy times.

When my kids were three and six, I revisited what I had many times before: whether it was right to reach out to my father after years of separation. My sister had told me he had pneumonia and, while fully recovered, was clearly getting older.

I had two children I loved deeply and wondered if it was wrong of me to withhold a relationship with their (now sober and seemingly more normal) grandfather and if somehow it was the more 'loving' thing to do to reestablish contact with him.

Being a clinical therapist at the time, I explored if I had done enough of my own work to feel safe and stable enough to connect with him. I reviewed all the layers (and layers!) of the trauma I had worked through (with my own therapist). I felt I was past being defined by it. I even understood that the abuse had occurred when he was drinking heavily and still in his own childhood trauma. I knew he was no longer drinking – though still in denial he had done anything – and had become an old man.

I thought I was ready to consider a relationship with him again.

I went to bed full of a sense of victory because I thought I knew I was ready to face the demon of my past and be a different person.

I woke up at 2:00 a.m. and threw up.

Violently.

Until my guts were empty.

I scheduled an emergency session with my therapist, and after some news telling, she said, "I want you to feel," she said. "What do you mean? I am crying my eyes out. I can't stop feeling!"

"No, wait. Just because you cry doesn't mean you actually feel sad. Just because you yell doesn't mean you feel angry." Whaaa?

I share with you now the greatest teaching of my mentor and guide and one of the most life changing discoveries in my own healing path:

There is a difference between 'being' the feeling and actually 'feeling' the feeling.

Many ways you have been told you were 'emotional' by crying or sighing or even yelling were actually just ways you were identifying with – and so being – the feeling rather than processing it. This is where the expression 'acting out' becomes so powerful. Rather than 'feeling' mad, you 'act it out' by yelling. Rather than feeling sad, you 'act it out' by crying uncontrollably.

Note: This does not mean that yelling or crying are wrong. On the contrary, they may be just what you need. But first let's get this principle down, and then we'll come back to that in Chapter 9 when I tell you about release.

By the way, remember how feelings are dynamic, and in flow? Well, a post script to my story is three years later, I revisited the possibility of reaching out to my father. And I discovered I actually felt calm. No nausea. In fact, it felt almost easy. I currently have a quiet and polite (albeit internally complex) relationship with him, and I am glad.

PRACTICE FEELING

Can you sit back and instead of becoming the feeling, hold some space for it?

Try this. Read the instructions, then put the book down.

Sit back right now and remember the last time you felt full of feeling – maybe you were crying, or yelling. Can you remember?

Now close your eyes. Imagine for a moment what that feeling might look like – give it a color or a shape. Does it have a sound? Become acquainted with it.

Now in your mind's eye, sit next to it. Shoulder to shoulder. As if you were peeking out the corner of your eyelids or looking down a street corner, can you see what it is doing? Saying? Let it show itself to you.

Now. Let it come closer, or go closer to it. Can you sit shoulder to shoulder? Can you hold it? Gently? With compassion? Can you let it jump up and down or rage or yell or storm? Without judgment? Can you promise to hold space for that feeling as long as it needs to express itself? Can you stay committed to holding and listening and allowing that feeling as long as it takes?

Because that feeling is you, and you matter.

Someone walking by might see you and not know a thing about what is inside of you right now. You might even look like you are meditating.

That is feeling the feeling rather than being it.

Go back to that time with Lydia, my therapist. She had me sit back, get comfortable in my seat, and "make space" for the nausea. When I tried to give it a color, it seemed red, with streaks of green. I could see it like a hot snake curled along my belly. I could feel my jaw was tight, and I felt my fingers curl into fists. It felt like I was getting ready for a fight or to defend myself.

"Hold open your arms big enough to bring that feeling in."

When I did, that hot red feeling exploded into a burning volcano, and I felt a rage like I never had.

Just the possibility of reinitiating contact with my father had unknowingly triggered a rage response from my intelligent body system.

The rage had come out as nausea – and literal vomit – because I had not known how to listen to how I felt (i.e feel!) about the actual possibility of seeing my father again.

In this case, my anger was both at my father for what he had done but also at myself for almost abandoning the boundaries I had worked so painfully hard to set.

My feelings – the nausea – showed me what my busy analytical, well-intentioned, wanting-to-be-a-good-mom-stellar-therapist mind could not.

Now, let us take a moment and consider that all of this can be enormously hard thing to do

The rage at my father was almost inaccessible to me because it was so overwhelming and scary. If it had been 'easy' to access, I would have known that as soon as I started to consider whether or not to see him.

And this is why we do this practice: to practice tolerating and allowing the feeling. When we allow the feeling, we allow access to that unique you – to your soul.

THE THINKING

You know the back and forth between wanting to like your body and what you actually think.

The thoughts are sometimes the obvious, "Ugh, my stomach is fat." And sometimes they are more subtle and insidious, like Kathy's, "I will find love if I lose twenty pounds." What becomes overwhelming is when what you think becomes what you feel.

You think your stomach looks fat, and so now your stomach feels bloated, distended, and aching.

Your thoughts become almost impossible to separate from how you feel.

You may know that body shame is somehow not okay, but with the judgment-thoughts coursing through your mind, it is almost impossible to believe.

And so you have a choice: suffer feeling bloated, and gross, and thinking you are unlovable, or check out. Get numb. Disassociate. Eat. Drink. Shop. Daydream. Anything to not feel how bad things feel right now.

Now, you need your mind. Of course you do! But for most of us – and especially for those of us who have a hard time staying in our bodies – the mind can do all kinds of neat and fancy tricks to keep us out of our feeling state.

You tell yourself there are reasons – good reasons! – to not heed how you feel. It's messy. It's childish. It's selfish.

You want to be a good mother, friend, or lover. You want to be the best daughter, friend, and sister.

And so you learn to ignore and keep away, and clamp down what you actually feel because to feel – and follow what you feel – puts you at risk of making waves and not being the 'good' person you are working so hard to be.

It is also worth noting here that if you grew up in a traumatic background (Remember your ACE score from Chapter 5), feeling was exceptionally challenging because there was nothing / no-one there to catch you – or it was an infrequent container at best – to teach you how to have the feeling move though you.

There was no space for your own nervous system regulation.

It made perfect sense at that time to check out of the building (the body) because it felt so bad and there was no one there to help find the better.

There was no one to say, "Hey, what you feel is so right! Your rage, your hurt. All that is moving through you is saying something about what is happening around, and to, you." And without that container, there was no time to mitigate, to process, and get through it.

Instead, you shut down, shut up, and turned off.

At least, you thought you did. But the feelings never stop. They just stay hidden or repressed and out of touch.

And without that outlet, the feelings back up into an overload.

And then, you are touched or want to be intimate, and it is like a firebrand pushing you to open up and feel.

Or you eat, drink, shop, daydream, whatever! to stay as far away from the overload as you can.

And inevitably, the true You – in that beautiful, fully-functioning Body – protests, but has nowhere to go with the justifiable anger and sadness within, and so loops back into self blame.

For most of us, when we are little, we are told – implicitly or explicitly – to button up, shut up, or get over it. How many of us learned somewhere that some feelings really weren't okay? Or at least less okay?

You learn that there are 'negative' emotions – the ugly, too demanding ones. But isn't that really because those are the ones that are hardest to tolerate?

Often the ones that are hardest to tolerate are the ones that show you what we need.

Anger is a boundary.

Sadness shows you what you feel you are losing and so what is valuable to you.

Feelings as themselves have no moral value. They are simply what they are: expressions of the self, communicating to you eloquently, elegantly, powerfully, and intelligently.

Have you ever felt you wanted to scream, rage, cry as long as you needed with no consequence? Wouldn't it be nice to have your friends and partners sometimes let you carry on – and make no attachments or interventions – just let you cry or yell it out with no reaction? It's almost hard to imagine, isn't it?

Goodness, my own children – after how many tries on my part – have felt my own frustration, impatience, or despair when their big feelings were inconvenient, overwhelming, or just annoying.

We all find places we don't tolerate or feel are 'too much.' Fair enough. Sure, listening to a child screaming is exhausting and no fun. But why?

How much of that is because we feel like we have to fix it, negotiate with it, or make it better?

What would happen if we allowed the feeling to just be?

I am not talking about giving in to a temper tantrum or marinating in sorrow for the sake of it. I am talking about sitting quietly and watching it flow like a river.

A RIVER

Feelings are dynamic. No moment is fixed.

What a relief to realize that every moment is dynamic. When you let loose your rigid protection against what you feel, and simply watch it, you discover that what you feel shifts.

It is the law of the universe that nothing can be destroyed, and nothing stays the same except love.

In the language of yoga, the only thing that stays the same is Love.

In Sanskrit, the language of yoga, the suffix "pra" means that which stays constant. The root "na" means to connect with. Prana, often used as the word for breath, means connecting with that which stays constant. And the only thing that stays constant is Love.

Perhaps this is what you call God, Spirit, Self, or Science. You name it what feels most true to you.

But there is a force which animates you and which is fixed, regardless of what moves around it. And you have a real, deeply personal connection with it – certainly your breath (more on this Chapter 9) but also you as an entity and as a unique being.

Knowing this will help you navigate the field of your feelings.

Whatever its name, everything else is impermanent. Think about it.

I know sometimes it feels as if you actually felt the feeling, you might never get over it. If you cried as much as you wanted to, you worry you might never stop crying.

But I can promise you the tears will not last forever. And what's even more exciting, when you make space for the feeling to flow, you become able to actually watch them shift and evolve.

Remember my volcano? When I really sat with it – I mean, really, really sat with it – I could see that moment to moment, breath to breath, the volcano was not static but changing. Prepared to stay with it as long as it took, I then found out that simply by showing up for it, I could feel those flames extinguish.

Nothing stays the same.

Jeff came to me following an extremely painful break up. He had been wildly in love with his girlfriend and imagined spending the rest of their lives together. When she broke up with him, it devastated him. After two months of lethargy and feeling uninspired at work, he came into my office desperate to feel better.

We did the Practice of Now, and Jeff immediately connected to the grief he felt so actively for months. At least, he connected to what he identified as his feeling; the tightness in the chest, the heaviness in his limbs, the tears. As we explored the range of sensations, he also identified shame, guilt, and a sense he shouldn't be grieving someone who "didn't want him." Furthermore, he could feel a terror that if he let himself be sad at his loss, it must mean that somehow he deserved to be left.

After some more of the Practice, I offered that he might make some space to "hold and allow" the feeling. It was clear we did not have time for the full expression in our single session – he was despondent. But he was willing to see what it would be like to let himself fully feel – and hold – the misery for as long as it would take. The weekend was coming up, and so he agreed to see what would open if he cleared his calendar and prepared to just let it flow.

The following Monday, Jeff came in and reported sitting in his big armchair Saturday morning. He brought over a box of tissue, a big fluffy blanket, and thought about his old girlfriend. He cried. And then cried harder. He held his arms out wide and welcomed all of it.

One hour passed. His eyes became puffy; his nose clogged.

Another half hour passed. He cried. How could he survive this for days?

And then another twenty minutes passed – not fighting the feeling, just watching it flow.

And then. It stopped.

As will whatever feeling is moving through you right now. Say hello to it because it will not be the same in ten minutes, and it deserves your acknowledgment.

THE WITNESS BODY

There is a concept in Vedic yoga which says that the self is made in layers, or "sheaths," (Koshas). At the true center is pure love, or God, or Self (Atman).

From outside to in, the first layer is anamaya kosha. This is the physical body, the "food stuff" of which we are made.

Then comes the manamaya kosha, the mind or mental body.

Then comes the breath body, or pranamaya kosha. This body actually has the ability to travel through all layers of the self – from the physical body to the true self (Atman).

Then comes the glorious and powerful witness body: the vijnyamaya kosha.

This sheath body is a truly magical one. As it is the layer closest to the true self, (Atman, God), it touches some of those properties of pure love.

The witness consciousness operates thusly: by allowing the witness of the "what is," you start the process of not being it. In other words, you have to be far enough apart in order to "see."

Remember the volcano-holding arms?

When you step back from being the feeling and instead allow the feeling, you gently untangle the mind from its perception of what it thinks you are.

And the mind wants to stay fixed, to stay safe, and will tell you how it thinks things need to be (in order to feel in control).

Family, society's expectations, old hurts and fantasies about how it all could be push your capacity to be present with the what is.

When we allow the witness with compassion, we tap into that spiritual immune system (Chapter 4).

My darling, it is time to recognize you are worth the effort of feeling. It is time to recognize that the feeling has been in you this whole time and that some of the suffering you are in is because you have not given yourself the space to listen to and care about it.

The genius of you is accessed by tapping into what you feel.

I know it is scary. I know it may seem like if you do, things may fall apart. You are so used to staying above and outside of your heart. But it is time to come home back to you. Are you ready?

CHAPTER 7

YOUR BODY

In this chapter, it is time for you to go deeper into your relationship with your body. It is no longer enough to just witness the story you told yourself; it is time to move toward love.

You've gotten to this point in the Practice to show you that the way you are experiencing this moment has intelligence and information in it.

Start just where you are.

Go deeper into the moment.

This practice is called The Practice of Now because the whole world – the infinite, spacious, complicated world – is right now.

And you are both a part of it and the whole thing itself.

Start right where and how you are – with compassion.

Start by considering that there is nothing wrong with you. That in fact you are perfect. If this feels just too alien and out of reach, how about considering the *possibility* you are perfect. And if not in this lifetime, maybe the next. Try this out: I am open to the possibility that in this lifetime or the next I may consider that there is nothing wrong with me."

This practice teaches you what you already know and connects you to who you already are.

Many of us have a hard time with (genuine) compassion. It is so easy to want to improve or fix ourselves and see all the ways we are imperfect and not quite what we want to be.

So how do you remedy that?

You connect to the compassion that is already inside of you.

How do you do that? Breathe.

BREATHING AS AN ACT OF LOVE

There is no greater expression of compassion than your breath.

This compassion is the first step of your practice.

Your breath does not care who you are or what you have done. It does not care if you are the CEO of a Fortune 500 company or a boy caught up in crime. It does not care if you are young or old or fat or thin. It does not care if you are the best wife or the nicest friend. It does not care if you want to be touched tonight or you want to be alone.

It feeds you and cleanses you no matter what.

It considers you to be such a valuable investment; it will never abandon you. Even when you try to resist it, it will have its way. Even when you try to keep it all in and hoard it in one gulp, it stays steady and with you.

It does not sneak off to care for someone else. It cares for you.

Go on. Try. Just try holding your breath. Doesn't it eventually insist on being let go? And how about not inhaling? Seriously. Try it. Take an inhale. Let it go. Then wait. See how long you cannot breathe in.

Feel your heart rate rise? Feel a pressure in your temples? Feel hot? Feel panicked or mad? Well, all of that is you and your breath calling back to itself, and saying "I must be." You are that important.

By being like your breath, you connect to the truth of who you are: unconditional love.

Know that you have this technology at hand at every second. This compassion is what you actually are.

Breath reminds you that you are worthy. It is an act of love.

You are breathed whether or not you are the size you think you should be or even the person you think you should become. From wherever you believe your breath sources, that force provides you with every inhale and every exhale.

You are breathed whatever your name, job, or gender. Every inhale, breath says, "Here, here is what you need." Every exhale, breath says, "Now, let it go. Rinse out. I promise that if you do, there will be more for you. As much as you need."

From the moment of your birth to the day you die, Breath reminds you that you are connected to a force that is telling you yes.

Yes, you are worthy. Yes, you matter. Yes, exactly the way you are is just right.

And whether you would like to see that as simply a miracle of science or direct proof of a force beyond biology, it is real.

In yoga, the word for breath is "prana." The prefix "pra–" means "that which does not change." "Na" is to "connect or join with." The word for breath means "connecting to that which does not change."

And the one thing that does not change is Love.

Love is all there is.

What is Love? Love is the universal principle that you matter. Love is the source and sustainer of all things. It is the force that guides the Universe into its complicated, utterly perfect expression of itself.

Love does not mean pretty, easy, or anything other than that it wants the best from itself. It wants to expand and evolve and bring all of us with it.

Love says there is nothing wrong with you. Love says the struggle you are in right now is the place that you can enter into a more profound and holy experience with yourself. That in fact, the experience of yourself is exactly what you need to make your way back to the One that you are.

The desire to blame or prevaricate or push away – from yourself – is what keeps you from Love.

Every time you push away from the experience you are having of the self, you are pushing away from Love.

All that chatter or worry that you are wrong or broken only separates you from the magnificence of you.

Everything makes sense. You make sense.

Lean into your feelings. Care about your concerns. Embrace the anger and the sad and the fear. Bring them all to the table and introduce each to the other. Nothing about you is a mistake. They all have something to add to the conversation. Let all of you become the kingdom.

Beth was a young dancer who had a successful business in marketing. She was making well over six figures a year and actively being sought by recruiters. She came to me because she felt the edges of an old eating disorder – unhappy with her body and anxious much of the time.

After a body scan and taking inventory, Beth connected to a tightness in her chest, and a "yucky feeling" in her stomach. After breathing quietly, and making space for the sensation, her feeling shifted to "hot pokers" along her low belly.

After practicing "holding the volcano," she identified the familiar sensations of perfectionism with stories of how her father had raised her.

Beth recognized that she was in the grips of a familiar need to be perfect. She was working at her job even when she was tired – and, significantly – even when she didn't like what she was doing.

She remembered being a teen in high school and in varsity basketball and being told by her father she needed to do fifty sit ups and push-ups before she went to bed when they were on vacation. It was clear – he said it explicitly – that if she didn't, she was not winner material and would let the team down. Beth didn't want to disappoint her father or her team, so despite being on vacation and despite being exhausted after a day swimming and hiking, she dropped and exercised.

Now, in our sessions, Beth was at first able to connect some of the sensations of "hot pokers" with how the incident made her feel. But what was transformational was the recognition that the reason she did that was she was afraid of losing her father's affection, support, and, ultimately, love.

With beginning to understand the source of that "perfectionism" at all costs – especially the needs of her body – and feelings – Beth was able to begin to make conscious decisions about what she – and her body – really felt and needed. Within a year, she left the marketing business altogether and has opened a successful holistic retail shop and is happily engaged to a lovely, loving man.

But she had to:

1. Feel what was in her.
2. Stay with her feeling (anger, fear, resistance)
3. Then, change her relationship to it

LOVE BREATH

Read these instructions, then put the book down.

Find a comfortable seat.

Feel your feet on the ground. Bring your attention to the skull and see it like an empty, white dome.

Now notice that you are, in fact, breathing. Just watch the rise and fall of your breath with the curiosity of watching a show. Where does your body lift when you inhale? How about when you exhale? Can you notice what part pulls in and lowers down?

There is nothing to fix. Remember, breath doesn't have a score card, or a grade. It believes in you one hundred percent.

Now, when you have a sense of the directions and qualities of your breath cycle, see if you can grow it – even just a little. Not to force, just to expand gently.

Do this three times.

Now, as you take your next inhale, can you bring the air deeper into the belly? Let the exhale just do what it will. Pause as much or as little as you want between the breaths.

Do this three times.

Wonderful.

Now. Take those three belly inhales, but when you exhale, pause and purse your lips to exhale. And here's the key: see how long you can make your exhale.

Do this three times.

Great. You are ready for the final step.

These last three breaths you will take at your own pace.

There is a phrase in Sanskrit, "So Hum," which loosely translates to "I am." It is a beautiful phrase because it so definitively says what the Practice of Now offers: everything is right here. You need look no further that the right now for all you need – not even to your name or who you think you have been or are trying to become.

When you inhale, silently repeat to yourself either "I" or "So." When you exhale, silently repeat to yourself either "am" or "Hum." Done.

Next Step.

BODY SCAN

Please visit my website http://www.janetfarnsworth. com for a free audio version of the below meditation.

During this meditation, you will harness ways of connecting to yourself without judgment, and instead, with compassionate witness.

COMING INTO THE ORDINARY

If you are doing this on your own, read these instructions through to the end, then try to commit them to memory, as you will eventually want to close your eyes. Another option is to read them into your phone, make an audio message, and play it back. Be sure not to rush through. You want to give yourself as much time as you need.

PART 1:

Find a comfortable seat.

Bring your feet to the ground.

Take three love breaths.

Look around. Take note of what is on the walls, the color and texture of the floor. See where the ceiling, floor, and door are. The animal body needs to know how to get in and how to get out.

When you feel that you have truly looked all around you, bring your gaze right in front of you.

Keep your eyes open but your gaze soft. Can you see what you see out the corner of your eyes? Colors of the floor? Maybe what you saw a moment ago is blurry or out of view. Perfect.

Just see what you see in this way.

Now. Gently close your eyes. You are going the same direction, from out to in. Now, instead of what is around you, notice what is in you.

But stay ordinary.

Take note of where your bones are.

If you were in first grade and had been asked to trace your body on the ground on a big piece of paper, where would your head, shoulders, arms, and legs be?

Can you just take note of where you bend and where you are straight?

Start at the empty, white dome of the skull and trace down though the body.

Good. Just like that.

When done, gently open the eyes and read the next step.

PART 2:

Now, same first grade assignment but a bit more to draw.

Notice that there is some mass over those bones. I don't want you to think about what they look like, just notice how they feel.

Start at the dome of the skull and begin at the scalp. You will trace your wazzy from the head, to the neck, shoulders, arms, hands, chest, belly, back, hips, bottom, legs – front and back, all the way to the feet.

Is some part feeling heavy? Or light? Is there a tingling or a tightness? How about a sharpness or a dull ache?

Just notice the sensations in those muscles, these parts, over the bones. When you notice a spot, just take note or leave a kind of mental post-it or map pin, then continue on.

Map this landscape of you. Take as long as you need.

When done, gently open the eyes and read the next and final step.

PART 3:

Place your feet on the ground.

Take three love breaths.

You will close your eyes and come into the ordinary as above.

But this time when you begin at the scalp, allow your first grader to open up to her imagination and see and draw whatever arises.

You may find a garden behind your left ear or a dog crouched in your hip. There may be colors or shapes or stories from the past.

Stay in your active imagination here.

Welcome whatever the body has to show you. You do not need to pull or fix or understand. Simply watch and allow.

When something arises, simply take note – tag the post-it or place the map pin – and continue. Head to foot.

This is it. And it is everything.

In a private session, this might be where we would pause and explore what has arisen. But while you are doing this practice on your own, I want you to have the option to keep going. It may be that doing the three-part scan connects you to what wants your attention to heal or care for. If so, this is a good time to journal or meditate or find someone to process what has come up.

But if you want to continue, follow along.

The more you learn to tolerate the sensations and

experience of the moment, the more you can open to the wisdom of the moment.

What is in your body? What treasures of information and guidance are there?

Moshe Feldenkrais, a brilliant scholar and scientist from Israel in the mid twentieth century, lived at a time when polio was ravaging a generation. If not outright killing children, it was leaving hundreds or thousands vulnerable to paralysis and being "crippled." Mr. Feldenkrais was desperate to find a way to help these victims walk or to regain or maintain the mobility they did have.

Feldenkrais discovered that by slowing movement down, the children's autoimmune – personal biology – helped repair itself.

By having children move to the point where their mobility would stop and then pause, their bodies seemed magically to restore and gain back some movement and mobility.

You get to harvest Mr. Feldenkrais' wisdom, practice that witness consciousness, and recognize that as you become more interested in the what is – where is your range of motion? – you discover that your body has the wisdom to know how it can expand and release old patterns.

So right from the get-go, release your judgment about what you are about to find. What you find just now, and it is perfect.

MAPPING THE BODY

Adapted from Rudolf von Laban's *Laban Movement Analysis:*

1. Take a walk around the room you are in. Walk for about two to three minutes.

2. Stop and reflect. Notice.

3. Okay. Now walk again. Even more slowly. After about a minute, start to change directions. Go sideways. The back ways. Then maybe in a circle. Now speed up. Walk again in different directions but faster.

4. Then pause. Again, what part of your body is initiating movement? Let yourself be surprised by what you find. Is it your legs? Arms? Jaw?

5. Now, find a posture to be still in. Any posture. Let your body pick it. You can be standing upright or lying in a ball. Let yourself just spontaneously find a shape to stay in. Notice: What is the shape of your body? As if you were drawing that picture of you in first grade, what design are you? Where are you in the room? What direction are you facing? What level/height have you chosen? What orientation have you picked? Perfect. Take a few breaths, and if you were lying down, stand up.

6. Go through this cycle at least one more time, but this time for five to ten minutes. You can stay with the walking or let yourself move freestyle. Allow yourself to move whatever direction you feel called and

at whatever speed. This is your opportunity to 'run a diagnostic' on the state of your body. It is okay to be messy, to change your mind, to not have any of it make sense. In fact, the more you can find some spontaneous and authentic movement, the better.

This time, before you go again, after three to five minutes of "just moving" (like a warmup), see if you can notice features of your movement while you are moving. Note: The below questions are guidelines. You may answer all of them, or you may have questions of your own. As long as you are staying interested in your body in motion, you are 100 percent doing this right.

- What body part(s) initiate movement?
- What shapes is your body taking?
- When you take a movement, does it stay in one area of your body, or can you feel it spread through you to other body parts?
- What is the force of weight where?
- Where do you change from heavy to light?
- What area in the room are you when you move in different ways?
- Do you turn your back to the door or always face it?
- Do you stay mostly up and down (vertical), or are there parts that move horizontally, or in zig zags?
- How much space do you take up?

- Is there a part of your body that you are always using? How about those that you use rarely or never?
- What is happening to your face?

This last time. Find that shape to rest in and do one last check in with anything you notice – from the ordinary to the sublime.

Allow the breath. Allow the body scan. Allow you.

All of these practices are practice to open you to you. There is no goal other than that.

The more you can tolerate the sensations and experiences of the moment, the more you can find the infinite expansion and liberation of the moment too.

The answers are in you. The experience you want to have with your body – the self image, the touch you want to be able to receive – is already who you are.

You just are practicing caring about what is in you so you can find out better what is keeping you from receiving what you want.

It may be that what you want is not what you thought it would be.

CHAPTER 8

YOUR AWAKENING

Now that you have 'arrived' in your body and practiced some nonjudgmental witness and awareness, it is time to go to the next step and begin to open to the vitality that is within. This chapter is about starting to turn your body on.

Remember, this is not about being selfish, this is about being what you already are. It is about being you and being love.

Modern yoga has become almost strictly about movement. For those of you who love the true, ancient practice of yoga, sometimes this can be frustrating. The eight-limbed practice of yoga – which speaks to the moral compass, honest living, kindness, and the art of meditation – is so much more than learning to stand on one leg or get your foot to your ear.

But guess what. In this practice, I invite – no, push – you into your physical practice.

Because in the physical practice, you meet yourself in the most real ways.

This matter you inhabit – your body – is in fact the house for who you are (and remember, who you are is Love).

Celebrate it. And celebrate it by starting to move it.

The Radiance Sutras, ancient texts called the Vijnana Bhairava Tantra,* are your invitation back home.

Understood to be a love song between Shiva, creator of the Universe, and Shakti, energy of the Universe, the sutras artfully describe what Life – (your Body!) – actually is.

You are going to use their words as anchors and inspiration, understanding that right now you may feel as far away from the poetry as the desert to the ocean. It's alright; all you have to do is listen.

YOUR SPINE IS YOUR CENTER

*"There is a current of love-energy that flows
Between Earth below and Sun above.
The central channel of your spine is the riverbed.
The streaming is as delicate and powerful
As the tingling touch of lovers.
Entering here,
Radiance arches between above and below.
Your who attention resting in the subtle,
Vibrating in the center of the spinal column,
Tracing this current between Earth and Sun,
Become magnetism relating all the worlds."*
– Radiance Sutrras, v. 12 Translated by Lorin Roche

Remember those tantra yogis? Remember whatever is in the cosmos exists in you? This is called the principle of correspondence.

That means that the forces of nature – the stars, the elements, the wind itself – has a vibration. And as you are microcosms of those forces, it means those vibrations are also in you.

(Vibration is such a wacky word, isn't it? But 'vibration' is actually science!)

We know that energy is actually in motion. Cells vibrate. One working definition of life includes the property of movement. So it makes sense that everything that lives – including what you are – is vibrating in some kind of shared frequency. To be in relationship with them is to be in resonance.

For the rest of the chapter, you will learn specific practices to help you to be in resonance with specific, positive energies which will assist you to feel comfortable not just with, but in, your amazing body.

The first practice will be to awaken and enliven your spine.

Chakra Cleansing & Balancing Mudras & Mantras

LAM   ROOT CHAKRA
MULADHARA
(SURVIVAL)
Base of Spine,
on Perineum
 Thumb & index fingers
touch. Arms Straight,
hands on knees.
Chakra Sound...
Long: L-A-A A-A-M

VAM SACRAL CHAKRA
SWADHISTHANA
(CREATIVITY)
Hips
 Place Hands in your lap
with your palms faring
upwards, right palm
resting on top of left.
Chakra Sound...
Long V-A-A-A-M

RAM   SOLAR PLEXUS
CHAKRA
MANIPURA
(WILL POWER)
Two-Inches Below
Naval
 Place Hands between your
heart and your stomach.
Chakra Sound...
Long R-A-A-A-M

YAM   HEART CHAKRA
ANAHATA
(Love)
Heart
 Right Hand:
Index finger & thumb touching
at Heart Centre. Left Hand
in same Mudra resting on
the Knee. Chakra Sound...
Long Y-A-A A-A-M

HAM THROAT CHAKRA
VISHUDDHA
(EXPRESSION)
Throat
 Hand by Stomach, fingers
interlaced & thumb tips
touching. Focus on
Throat Chakra.
Chakra Sound...
Long H-A-A-A-M

AUM   THIRD EYE
CHAKRA
AJNA
(INTUITION,
WISDOM)
Third Eye
 Hands in front of the lower
part of your breast. Middle
fingers stand up tips
touching, other fingers
bent at first joint as shown
Chakra Sound
Long A-A-A-U-U-M

ANG CROWN CHAKRA
SAHASRARA
(SPIRITUAL
CONNECTION)
Crown
 Hands in front of your
stomach, fingers
interlaced. Little fingers
pointing upwards
Chakra Sound...
Long A-A-A-A-N-G

SEVEN CHAKRA AWAKENING

For this exercise, make sure you have some privacy and quiet.

Over a thousand years ago, tantra healers and scholars recognized that anatomy is not only something that can be seen, sliced, and dissected, but in fact, is also energetic. Those scholars identified how some of these energies live in you and intermingle. These pathways are called "nadis," and you have 72,000.

Miraculously, they spiral around and through, both beginning and ending, in epicenters along the spine. These create a spiral of energy which we call the chakras.

(I know. You either know this all too well, or it's just too weird. But stay with me.)

Remember that you are in correspondence with the Universe. The chakras are no different – in fact, they are themselves in correspondence.

Each anatomical energy center – at a specific space along your spine – reflects and vibrates the energy which is inside and outside of you. This energy can be experienced in sound, color, and shape.

Where you bring your attention is where your energy will go. The yoga tradition teaches that Prana – life force – actually 'rides' the breath and will go to wherever you bring your awareness.

This is some of the same thinking of the Law of Attraction, which says that there is a magnetic power of the universe that draws similar energies together.

This law states that every thought is made up of energy which has its own unique frequency. And when this frequency radiates out into the Universe, it naturally interacts with the material world. And so, as your thought radiates out, it attracts the energy and frequencies of like thoughts, like objects, and even like people, and draws those things back to you.

MEDITATION PRACTICE

For this exercise, you will engage your senses and your awareness to awaken the infinite energy of the world which travels along your spine. It involves three parts:

1. Hold Hand Mudra. (Mudra = Gesture)
2. Visualize Corresponding Color
3. Listen to/Chant Bij Mantra, or, Listen to/Chant Corresponding Affirmation. The "Bij" – meaning "seed" – mantra is said to be the sonic vibration (sound!) of the corresponding chakra. If you prefer, you can also chant the English affirmation which represents the positive energy of the chakra.

For listening or chanting, search any main music library/app, and look up "Chakra Meditation" or "Chakra Bij Mantra." There are many; find one that suits you. For reference, here is one version that I use and enjoy.

Mantra Seed Sounds Vol. 2 Chakra Bijag, Mantrapoly
For each chakra, for one to eleven minutes:

1. Bring your hands to the corresponding mudra.
2. Play the track of the bij mantra, or chant the affirmation.
3. Close your eyes, and visualize the chakra in your body (literally imagine it in your body), and see the corresponding color.

This is how you awaken the energies of your spine as an expression of the energy of the infinite you. In doing, you awaken to the vitality and joy in your body – and you!

I know this might seem weird at first. But since no one is watching, just go ahead and give it a try!

FIVE SENSES AWAKENING EXERCISE

*"The senses declare an outrageous world –
Sounds and scents, ravishing colors and shapes,
Ever-changing skies, iridescent reflections –
All these beautiful surfaces Decorating vibrant emptiness.
The god of love is courting you, Light as a feather.
Every perception is an invitation into revelation.
Hearing, seeing, smelling, tasting, touching –
Ways of knowing creation,
Transmissions of electric revelation.
The deepest reality is always right here.
Encircled by splendor, in the center if the sphere,
Meditate where the body thrills
To currents of intimate communion.
Follow your senses to the end and beyond
Into the heart of space."*
– Radiance Sutras, v. 9 Translated by Lorin Roche

There is an ancient Hindu practice called a puja. A puja is a ritual traditionally offered as a blessing for a deity or an act of worship.

Today, you worship the miracle of your body. Just as it is.

There can be something terribly artificial about saying you like yourself when you decidedly don't. I'd even go so far as to say there is something potentially counterproductive when you do. As if for every "I love myself" (when you feel the opposite) you inflict on yourself your instinctive response of "actually I don't love myself."

Let me be clear: you are engaging in this puja as an exercise for what is already in you. This is just by nature of being human. You have neither done anything to deserve it nor to be punished by it. This is simply honoring what is.

You may make this as elaborate or as simple as it suits you. You can make all kinds of preparation or quietly find a way to do this simply, easily.

Our goal here is to quite literally "turn up and turn on" the brilliance of your body – and for you to discover that you don't have to do anything to find it. You just have to pay attention to it.

For this exercise, make sure you have some privacy and quiet. The instructions are not fixed.

You may find you want to lengthen or modify the times. But please the first time do not shorten the minimum per sense.

To Prepare, find the following items:

- One pleasant smelling item. This can be a bottle of a lotion you like or perhaps a flower or an essential oil.
- One item to taste. This can be whatever you want. But hey – as long as you are putting something in your mouth, why not something you like?
- One item to listen to. You can play a track on the radio or your phone or stereo. Just be sure that if you choose the radio, it is to a station that you like and preferably doesn't have too many commercials. (Again, if you're going to listen to something, make it something you want to hear.)
- One item to touch. (If it's your cat or dog or anything alive, make sure it can't bolt or leave you!)
- One mirror. Yep. I want the thing you look at/see to be you. I realize this may be a big trigger but hang in here with me. If you are looking to "wake up the body," guess whose body that is? Yep. That woman you are looking at it in the mirror. And if it turns out that all you can do when you see your reflection is criticize and find the flaws, practice your witness consciousness (remember vijynanamaya kosha?) and just keep breathing. You actively want to meet those places that are beating up on you and keeping you beaten down and rejected. (And besides, you get to interact with them more directly to change them in the next chapter.)

You are going to feel silly at first. You will want to deflect, and short circuit. Notice this, and don't back out. The deflection is exactly an expression of what you have already been doing with your body.

If it feels silly or too hard to consider yourself something to celebrate, consider that what you are honoring is the Divine in you. Not the ego or the fears but the best of you.

In fact, this is a ritual to awaken and connect to the part of your body that knows exactly how, when, and if you want to be touched. Consider it as an investment into the future and into your relationship. Remember, if you are not comfortable touching you, how can we expect you to be comfortable being touched by anyone else?

This is a ritual to awaken, and connect you, to you.

SMELL

"Forget all of your ideas about the body –
Its' this way or that way.
Just be with any area of it,
This present body,
As permeated with limitless space,
Drenched in freedom."
– Radiance Sutras, V. 23, Translated by Lorin Roche

1. Pick up your item to smell, then read this sutra either silently or out loud.

2. Now give yourself three to five minutes to inhale and exhale.
3. Just this.

TASTE

"Tasting dark chocolate,
A ripe apricot,
A luscious elixir –
Savor the expanding joy in your body.
Nature is offering herself to you.
How astonishing to realize this world can taste so good."
– RS, V 49, Translated Lorin Roche

1. Pick up your item to taste, then read this sutra either silently or out loud.
2. Now bring your item into your mouth. Feel it on your lips, then on your tongue. Hold it there for at least a minute.
3. For three to five minutes, chew – slowly – or suck, hold, and taste your item.

SOUND

"Immerse yourself in the rapture of music.
You know what you love. Go there.
Tend to each note, each chord,
Rising up from silence and dissolving again."
– Radiance Sutras, v. 18 Translated Lorin Roche

1. Begin with silence.
2. Then read aloud this sutra.
3. Find silence again.
4. Now play your track first quietly, then louder. Notice the difference in your body – vibration and sensation – when the music is quiet, then loud.
5. For three to five minutes play the track and simply notice everything you can about how it feels to listen.

TOUCH

> *"Attend to the skin*
> *As a subtle boundary Containing vastness.*
> *Enter that pulsing immensity.*
> *Discover that you are not separate*
> *From anything there.*
> *There is no inside,*
> *There is no outside,*
> *There is no other–*
> *No object to meditate upon that is not you."*
> – RS, V 25 Translated by Lorin Roche

1. Place your item next to you, then leave it.
2. Read the sutra silently or out loud.
3. Now bring your non-dominant hand to pick up the item. As you do, pay attention to the precise sensation on your skin, and when and if you can feel any pressure in your muscles, or in your bones.
4. Bring the item into your dominant hand.

5. For three to five minutes, press, roll, slide the item between the hands, along the arm, and anywhere else you would like to explore.

SIGHT

"If this is the nature of the Universal Self,
Then who is to be worshipped?
Who do I invoke, and who do I meditate upon?
To whom do I offer oblations, To whom do I sacrifice?
If everything is divine,
And consciousness merges with divine essence,
Then what happens to the distinction between worshipper
and worshipped?
RS Insight Verses, V 141

"Worship does not mean offering flowers.
It means offering your heart
To the vast mystery Of the Universe.
It means letting you heart pulse
With the life of the universe,
Without thought and without reservation.
It means being so in love
That you are
Willing to dissolve
And be recreated in every moment.
– RS Insight Verses, V 147

1. Pick up the mirror.
2. Before even looking, check in and notice and internal dialogue. Do not fix, just watch.

3. Bring mirror to your face.

4. What do you see? Can you look without judging? Can you trace the outline of your head without commenting? Can you look at and trace the shapes of what you see?

5. Eye gaze with yourself. This means just looking in your eyes for one to two minutes.

6. For three to five minutes, simply look at all you can of yourself without judgment.

THE SIXTH SENSE

The sixth sense, my love, is how you feel.

Feel free to practice "Coming into the Ordinary," or simply stay curious about what is happening in your heart.

Because that is what helps you start to move.

STARTING TO MOVE

A point of clarification on stillness versus stopping

As you deepen into the Practice of Now, you may find that what is most true for you is stillness. Still does not mean stopping.

Remember, as long as you are breathing, you are moving life energy and have a direct line to Love.

In fact, I want to share with you my own experience of stillness as a physical practice.

Several years ago, while doing my second 200-hour teacher training, the class was doing a module on ayurvedic doshas.

We learned that every person is made up of elements – specifically, earth, water, air, and fire. Most of us are born with a specific constitutional element, called a dosha.

The usefulness of knowing your dosha is so you can know what you need to balance it. For those of us who are vata or air, we need the balancing element of earth. Earth/water, or kapha element, to be balanced often needs a bit of fire to make sure we don't turn to mud and so on.

This is meaningful because when you know your primary element, you can track when you are out of balance – too much water/fire/air – and explore what you might need to balance yourself.

(If you want to learn more about it, just look up the words ayurveda and dosha.)

There are tests you can take to determine your element, and it was pretty clear pretty quickly I am pitta. This means constitutionally I incline to fire and power. Effort excites me, and I often have the strength to follow through. Though this can mean I get things done, it also can turn out of balance, and I overdo. When that happens, I become inflamed. This plays out as something as obvious as inflammation in the skin or acid in my tummy, but it also plays out in a relentless self-criticism (Gotta get better! Push on! No matter how like crap you feel).

Well, I was determined to be a really good student, and (apply all my fiery efforts to!) do less – the balance for my dosha. The instruction for me was to consider only doing three quarters of the practice, even one half, to see if I could soothe the heat in my body.

I settled onto my mat and awaited the instructions from our teacher.

At her first cue to step our right foot back, I decided to go slowly. Then she cued the left foot. I moved it slowly too. Almost right away she had us open up our arms, and engage our core strength. I think I barely lifted my hands up. Within two minutes, I missed some of her cues, only doing half of what she instructed.

And that was it. I sobbed. About ten minutes later, I think I curled up in child pose and let the class go by me. I think I may have cried the whole time. Just curled up, knees tucked under my chest, head cradled in my hands.

It was one of the most powerful, life-changing classes of my life.

And I only actually moved about eight minutes out of sixty.

The physical practice of yoga is really about sustaining the pose as a way to experience the now and meet the self.

The Practice of Now is really no different; you just get to add another variable to opening to the dynamic nature of the now – and of you.

Remember, moving can be internal; you can move while still.

The practice is for you to connect to the truth, to the essence of where and how Love (you) is leading you.

This is not for anyone else but you. We want to activate that Love, and "Turn you On."

MUSIC VERSUS SILENCE

Just a quick note to encourage you to do whatever feels best for you. If you have music that you love to listen to and it makes you feel like tapping your toes or even dancing, please put it on. But if you prefer silence, by all means do that.

I find that music has an enormous impact both on how I feel and how I move. Over time of cultivating this practice, you may find that it becomes less of a question and any music brings you closer to your vitality, but for now, I encourage you to play music that you know makes you happy and has a beat!

At this stage of the practice, we are gently offering our body its first invitation to dance. If you can remember being in middle school and going to a dance, my guess is you wouldn't have appreciated it if someone came and pushed you onto the floor.

Well, even if you are the first one to there at the party or club, we invite all of you to this dance – including your middle school you.

Let's start easy, gentle, with a good will.

FIRST STEPS

This exercise includes simple instruction for you to start to move.

You may want to record these instructions, or commit them to memory (if that is easy). The point is not to be perfect, or stay rigidly with any one movement. Actually the opposite, the point is to start to allow your body the experience of itself while in motion. You will find the first ten suggestions are specific, and designed to have you feel the specifics of your body's sensations. The last ten steps are suggestions for you to start to explore how you move in space.

Some of this may seem over-simple or dull. Do it anyway. Pay attention to the inner dialogue, and then stay with it. Stay with you. This is your practice.

1. Play your music (or stay in silence.)
2. Walk. Just walk.
3. Pause, and stand still.
4. Cross arms. Uncross. Re-cross. Let your arms rest at your side
5. Open your arms wide, then reach them behind you.
6. Pause, and stand still.
7. Take up space: five-pointed star. Separate your feet wider than your shoulders, and reach your arms out to the sky, in a wide, V shape.
8. Get small: a ball. Tuck into a tiny ball. Stay for awile, or let it go.
9. Five-pointed star again

10. Pause, and stand still.
11. Walk randomly around your space. Would you like to do this in time with the music? Or in between beats? How does your movement want to interact with the sound (or lack of it)?
12. Move up and down
13. Move sideways
14. Move backwards
15. Move in circles
16. Isolate body parts
17. Don't forget the head, neck, and face
18. Pause, and stand still.

Repeat with the music for five to ten minutes; Move, or dance in a way that feels natural and an honest expression of how you are feeling. There is no way to get this wrong. The way to get it right is already who you are.

Just move.

When you are done, do a quick body scan. Then, let it go.

We are not here to evaluate or interpret. We are here simply to be.

We are coming Home to you.

CHAPTER 9

YOUR INTUITION

I n this chapter, you will begin the process of refining your relationship to your intuition. Your intuition is your bridge to your inspired, live-out-loud, all-knowing, who-cares-how-I-look, or what-you-think-about-me Self.

Your intuition is what will allow your body to move naturally, which opens you to a sensuous experience of yourself, which in turn undoes the relentless criticism and self-hate. Move first. End hate second. This may feel a bit backwards, but I promise you it works. (By the way, can we give a little shout out to the word "sense-uous"?! As in come home to your senses, and come home to your sexy! Yes!)

But in order to find your inspired intuition, (i.e your natural sensuality!) you need to find and connect to your Yes and know your No. (Try saying that five times fast.). In other words, in order to feel the instinctive and awake You, you need to know what your boundaries are (your 'No'), and what your pleasure feels like (your 'Yes'). This is where the art of feeling gets even juicier.

In Chapters 4 to 8, you began this practice by beginning to consider the perfection of your body as a system – and that there is nothing wrong with it and nothing wrong with you. That, in fact, your body has flawless instinct and responds with great logic to your experiences. The trick now is to allow and understand better what experiences you are having.

Remember how in polyvagal theory/ACE scores/ understanding your brain, you found that experiences you had had created biological responses in your body?

And if somewhere your body has stored traumatic events or unexpressed (unfelt) feeling, then your body is going to respond as though that is still what is happening.

Well, those traumatic events and subsequent response systems have kept you in a loop of survival which has kept you from the natural, intuitive (and vital) genius in your body.

And it's time to re-establish relations with your Self again.

INTUITION

A useful and functional definition of intuition is "the ability to acquire knowledge without inference and/or the use of reason." The word 'intuition' comes from the Latin word 'intueri' which means 'to look inside' or 'to contemplate.' Instinct is key to your evolution.

Your job is to find out what is actually happening in your body and how to release whatever blocks/old events you may be still storing.

Now, there is an entire world of somatic therapy and somatic experiencing. I highly suggest pursuing outside support if, in fact, you do suspect you have stored trauma. You will learn more about this in Chapter 12.

The Practice of Now, meanwhile, takes a gentler, more sideways approach. We may not get to the root of the issue, but we can gently tug at it and start to de-tangle some of the knots you may be experiencing.

Your body is actually one radiant, Yes zone– and knows fully your power and your pleasure (your yes).

But somewhere, your relationship with your (perfect) body became less a pleasure zone and more of a battleground.

Somewhere, the yes that is (in) your body got obscured, stomped on, or hidden.

Most of us at some point in our development have them kind of mushed up and smashed together. We slowly learn that our instinct is not to be honored, and we will be loved better if we follow the no's which are assigned to us – either by our families or the culture around us. Our bodies are not our own. Goodness, it starts with potty training really – but just as particularly, it continues when we learn all the ways we must compromise our physical instincts.

Think about it. We all have had micro aggressions against our physical truths – our actual Yesses.

"Go to the bathroom now."

"Put your seat belt on."

"Smile."

"Say hello to Uncle Tom."

"Kiss Aunt Louise."

There are a hundred ways you were told not to honor the instinct and impulse of your deep physical knowing.

Carol is seventy-one years old and a sex therapist. She works with both men and women on awakening blocked sexuality. She is clear that most issue she deals with come from the micro aggressions against the body which begin in childhood. Over and over, she reports that most people have psychosomatic blocks against their own natural instinctive sexual agency because they have such restricted access to their intuitive knowing. Her work is to remove those blocks and free people to connect to their true instincts, and by doing, enjoy more gratifying sex lives.

As woman, we have complicated relationships (at best) with our bodies.

From the time you realized there were ways your body was supposed to look to be desirable, attractive, and then find love, you also found out there were things you could do or be which would make you undesirable.

Too fat? Too skinny? Too short? Too tall? Too white? Too black?

You have been drowned in images and expectations which insist you have to improve. Screw it. Who wants to be done with that nonsense? I know I do! How about you? But how?

WHEN NO IS YOUR YES

When I did my first 200-hour training, I was a really gung-ho, show-up-first, leave-last, do-the-assignment-to-perfection kinda student.

About two thirds through, we were scheduled for a session after discussing boundaries – both as practitioners and as teachers – and how to honor and attend to both.

After break, we came back to work a pose called 'bridge.' It involves lying on your back with knees bent, arms reaching down, and your butt in the sky. It requires glute and leg strength, and after a minute, you feel it. Well, one minute turned into three, and then into about five minutes. Let me tell you, five minutes is a long time pushing into your feet and, if you're like me, keeping a plenty big butt up.

The student teachers were all beginning to groan and grunt, and there was a general discussion of "this sucks" and "are you kidding me?" But then the five minutes became eight.

Well, something in me snapped. I suddenly didn't want to be really gung-ho, show-upfirst, leave-last, do-the-assignment- to-perfection kinda student. I was done.

And in that moment, my yes was one big, resounding no.

I put my butt back on the mat and crawled over to the side of the room, crying. I spent the next half an hour sobbing, snot rolling down my cheeks as my fellow students worked to maintain their bridge pose.

In that moment, my best yes was taking myself out completely.

SUZANNAH

Suzannah is a thirty-six-year-old successful, professional dance teacher. When she turned thirty, she developed neurological symptoms which affected her balance, stability, and muscle control. As a lifelong athlete and dancer, there were few things that could have been more devastating to her sense of order and well-being.

When she came to see me, her symptoms had become chronic, and she was diagnosed with dystonia. This affected not only her muscles but also some of her processing abilities and nervous system regulation.

Eager to not be limited by her disorder, she continued to swim and practice yoga regularly. While staying active, her symptoms seemed to reduce, but they continued to progress. Soon, she worked on being comfortable wearing leg braces.

And on she went.

She kept practicing yoga and even planned trips to visit Spain and Asia.

While clearly driven by an extraordinary love of life and determination not to let the diagnosis dictate her choices, in her Practice, she also recognized some other, more complicated patterns.

She was a gymnast as a child and had learned that no matter what – or at what cost – you got back up and carried on. Once as a child, she fell off a beam, landed on her head, and was told to get back on.

She remembered, too, how her family pretty much didn't want to know about anything uncomfortable or difficult, and she was expected – as were her siblings – to always act as if everything was okay.

Over time, Suzannah connected with the ways she accommodated her truths - how *she felt* - to keep the good will of those around her. She had learned that no matter what, she had to keep up or lose out: She had been trained to always say "yes," no matter how it made her feel.

Then, about a year into treatment, she went on a yoga retreat. In addition to the healing movement she craved, the retreat also involved a kind of breath work to stimulate the nervous system. Ever eager to keep up, she talked with the facilitator about whether to do it. Every fiber in her wanted to not feel left out, to not be different, to say "yes".

But Suzannah herself was different this time. Because she had done the work to explore and honor what she was feeling, something shifted from "do no matter what", to "do what is right, right now.". Suzannah realized that going to that particular event would be triggering and antagonizing for her nervous system. And for the first time since the development of her symptoms, she found her "No."

In her case, she wound up going to the retreat center pool and soaking in the water, watching the stars while the rest of the group did the breath work. She came back to the group when it was over.

But she had to face the fear of being alone, and in a very real way, challenge what had been a lifetime of accommodation. She had to find what her actual yes was. And yes for her in this case was a No.

By listening deeply to how she felt, Suzannah was able to discriminate the truth of her body's knowing, and make a choice that was best for her. When she came back from that pool and re-joined the group, she came back with integrity, and love.

How are you saying yes when you really mean no? Did you smile at the teacher when you really wanted to snarl? (Okay, how about just not look happy?)

Oh, of course we are social creatures and want to interact civilly. But for the purposes of this practice, I want you to be able to refine what your body says is a yes and no.

It is only when you determine your yes and your no that you will be able to act with integrity as who you truly are.

It's only when you do that you will be able to know – and communicate to your partner – what touch is good and what touch is not.

If there is some part of you that is still holding yourself in the way you either were explicitly told or that you taught yourself as a way to survive, let's get to know it.

WHEN NO MEANS NO, AND LEARNING TO LOVE IT

DANCING SHADOW: PART 1

In Chapter 8, you started to move and began to map your unique ways of moving.

Now, you are going to go the opposite direction. You want to find out how you don't move.

This is going to feel weird and super challenging. Welcome that fear – bring on the witch! Let her dance with you, and don't abandon her.

Put on some music you like that makes you want to move. But now I want you to move in.

1. The dumbest way you can imagine.
2. The most embarrassing way you can imagine.
   What would be the absolute worst way to be caught moving?

3. The worst / ugliest/ scariest / way you can imagine. How 'bad' can you be? Let your gut hang out. Be awkward. Stiff. Maybe drool or spit a little.

Remember, this is just for three minutes. You can do it!

I want you to just meet that part that until now has been the "bad" part of being in your body.

Don't give up. Be dreadful!

Then, just pause.

Just three more minutes.

Now that you have identified them, let them dance.

DANCING SHADOW: PART 2

Remember Betty, the thirty-two ballerina who hadn't trusted her body and discovered her father lingering around her edges, pushing her to do those sit-ups when she really wanted to go to bed?

After immersing herself into the Practice of Now, she became quite sophisticated at discerning what she was really feeling and learning to awaken her intuition. After about a year, she realized she was unhappy in her job in sales. While successful economically and socially in a high-status job, she realized she was staying in it as an obligation to her father. With time and practice, she heard quite clearly from her true intuition that she wanted to leave and start another career.

Her fears were both instinctive – money, safety, home – and more subtle (but still deep): disappointing her father. But she quit and opened her own business in holistic healthcare and is happier than she has ever been.

FIRE OF TRANSFORMATION

In this exercise, you will allow your body to do the work of release. Your mind does not even need to know explicitly what your body and intuition do.

This is an opportunity to finally release whatever has been keeping you from your Truth: Whether it be a Yes or a No, this is the time to rinse out what has been keeping you from knowing it.

Find a song without words that makes you want to move. I suggest a drumming song, such as James Asher's "Send in the Drums" from his Feet in the Soil album.

1. For six minutes, jump, shake, slide, shimmy, bounce, anything, but keep moving. Even if it just your arms, keep the body moving. Increase your heart rate. For six minutes, let the heat in your body rise.

2. As you do this, in your mind's eye, start to see a fire building. See the flames. Feel the fire burning hotter and hotter.

3. Now, at the seventh minute, imagine that you are releasing whatever is keeping you from your true (not the programmed) Yes. Is it a belief you have to play small or be perfect? Is it a fear you are too big? Just for this last minute, I want you to imagine you are casting it to burn in the fire.

4. Pause.

5. Rest.

FINDING YOUR YES

You've already done the preparation for this exercise with your Senses Awakening Series. Today I want you just to pick one of the sense which was actively pleasurable for you. A taste? A song? I want you to go back to that one thing. Just for five minutes. And track what it feels like to have pleasure. Feel it. Know it.

6. You are now ready to dance.

CHAPTER 10

LET LOVE MOVE YOU

When I started to dance at forty years old, I approached it in an entirely different way than when I did when I was a child and a teen in high school, even through college. Then, dance was about performance. It was about how I looked, and if I was doing the choreography the prescribed way.

When I started to dance again at forty, I was a mother and a wife, and I frankly didn't have much time or brain space to think about things like coordinated outfits or fancy steps. For me, it was about finding something fun to do when I was free and maybe getting some exercise.

I joined a local theatre group; my first production was *Cabaret*. I had a small part – not sure I even had a name – but I got to dance for the first time in maybe twenty years. I loved being with friends, getting away from the house for a few hours (guilty though I felt), and moving around to spectacularly fun music. But I hated the stress of having to learn steps. One, two, ball, switch. Turn. Hip shake. It was really a kind of torture. I was rotten at remembering choreography and always felt a bit behind everyone else.

At the same time, I went to a weekly event called Ecstatic Dance. The contrast was striking. At that event, the music would play, and That. Was. It. Any movement was alright. I could stomp or slide or wiggle or leap. There was no getting it right. I could move whatever the hell way I wanted to. And I loved it.

It was at those weekly events I came alive.

I want you to know that feeling.

But I am going to save you the fuss of finding a group or a place to go other than your own living room.

I want you to know what it is to tap into the fullness of your own experience and know what it is to not be afraid to "screw up" and "get it right."

Because guess what? There is no "right" in authentic movement.

You are already *all* right. I'm not trying to be cute. I am dead serious.

It is time for you to realize that everything you are is exactly as you should be. That includes the way you look and feel.

Your body is filled with wisdom, always working to bring you back to your own genius, always trying to tell you what is True. Listen.

Enough of making yourself small, and believing you are not supposed to feel (or be) who you are.

In fact, guess what? What you feel is exactly what is going to teach you how to move.

Remember how we figured out that you are an endlessly dynamic stream of feeling and sensation? Well all of that is now your choreography.

Have you seen the movie *Working Girl*? You know that scene where Melanie Griffith is vacuuming in her underwear? I remember seeing that and thinking to myself, "No way! I would never do that. I don't care if no one can see me – I can see me."

Are you worried about that? I get it. I do. Even to this day, I have to talk myself off the ledge any time I feel like I am going to be witnessed. I have to watch all the tiny – and big – criticisms that litter my mind when I see myself. I have to watch all the ways I want to 'fix' myself, and try to look 'right.'

I still have to remind myself that my worth is not in how I appear, but who I am. I still long to be seen and adored.

But really, who cares how you look when you dance by yourself? Who is watching you move? Just You.

Right now, you are now your own greatest judge, and most relentless critic.

It is time to give yourself a big, fat break, and let the critic have the afternoon off.

A few years into my movement workshops, a woman named Alisa came who was an experienced dancer and knew me from the ecstatic dance community. She was open and friendly and excited to be there because she loved to move.

She reported having some discomfort and stiffness in her hips but otherwise felt physically well. She was in a new relationship and was busy at work. Overall, she was just happy to be with us because she liked to dance.

We started with body scans and became familiar with how we wanted to move that night. We started slowly and with intention, but Alisa was ready and moving within minutes. She was strong, and fluid. (Though I actually make a point of not watching other dancers when I facilitate, I also keep my eyes out to make sure people are safe.) Alisa clearly had dance training and was bending, stretching, reaching, twirling. She was doing it all.

Well, that night we were going to explore our shadow sides and brought the movement and music to a slower beat. After some instruction, the group was encouraged to move in ways that, before then, we couldn't imagine doing. I saw Alisa kind of pause, almost bewildered – as if she couldn't imagine a way she hadn't already explored. Then, after about a minute, it was as if she transformed. Her movement became heavy, and choppy, and I can't think of a better word: awkward. She would lurch, and then go sideways. She stopped and started. She looked like she had never moved in her life.

After about ten minutes, she sat on the floor and sobbed. Big, wracking, snotty sobs.

She later said that she felt like she opened a whole new doorway into her soul and realized on some deep level how she still held on to the need to be pretty, accomplished, and all the things she thought her therapy had cured.

Can I tell you about Sheila too? Sheila is a cheerful woman of thirty-six who was born without arms. She has just two hands in her shoulder sockets. When she dances, she needs to have a chair at the edge of the circle because her legs get tired. (She also does karate by the way.)

How about Greg, who was paralyzed in a car accident, and loves to dance with his upper body?

Or our beloved friend and student Suzannah who has a neurological disorder and wears braces? She twirls and spins with the best of 'em.

Do you get the point?

You are no 'better or worse' than anyone else!

You are you, and You is who we want to invite to move.

THE "PRACTICE OF NOW"

"Dance is the hidden language of the Soul."
– Martha Graham

Please note you are not being asked to join the ballet or even to put on a tutu. In a way, you are not even really being asked to dance at all.

You are being asked to move in a way that is authentic to you.

And it gets even better! While authentic movement (dance) is your goal, that does not actually even mean you have to *move* your body.

Movement does not necessarily mean action.

Movement means connecting to the experience of the moment and then letting the moment express itself. In other words, the moment is the genuine expression of you..

If you breathe (and I know you do), you know that no moment is fixed.

One breath happens, then it is gone. Then, the next new one comes.

The Now is dynamic. Like a river, 'now,' by definition, moves. Constant, evolving. Sometimes quiet, sometimes loud. Sometimes smooth, sometimes choppy. The Now has a rhythm – one pulse to one pulse.

And as long as you are practicing a connection to that, you are dancing.

In PON: Let Love Move You, you have the opportunity to add in some music and let your unique rhythm make shapes, dips, and waves in the water.

In this way, you dance.

Dance is your nature, and it's time to dance. So how do we do it?

LET LOVE MOVE YOU

Read the below instructions, commit them to memory as you can, then put the book down. This Practice is to help quiet the mind, not tax it. If you cannot remember the steps, I officially give you permission to make something up. Just put that music on, and go. Let your intuition invent something to do with that music. There is an excellent chance that what you make up will be even better suited to what you need.

FIRST STEPS

1. Safe Place

Even when I facilitate in a large group – unless we are deliberately dancing together – I instruct people to not look at each other. This liberates us from that awful creativity-kill of comparison, as well as helps us go in and find the genius inside.

You need a safe space. Please note this does not just mean a physical space to move; this also means space created by time. Don't do this (at least the first time) when the kids are right outside waiting for you to come out or when your husband is waiting to talk to you about plans for the weekend. We can't settle into safety within ourselves when we have any distractions from without.

You only need a minimum of twenty minutes, but make them your own.

2. Compassion

You already did the work of practicing your witness, connecting to your body, finding the yes and the no, and releasing the blocks. Sure, we need to practice all of it over and over – you are a gorgeous, complicated, dynamic being! – but give yourself the credit of having done the preparation work to get here to this moment.

Most importantly, consider that whatever way you move you are right.

3. Music or Silence?

This one is on you, one hundred percent. I can share with you that in my experience music is a kind of tonic for the busy mind that already is reading this and trying to figure out how to control your Practice – whether to control it to make sure you don't mess up or to control it to make sure you win, but I promise you your mind is already well in the game. Let's give it something to rest in. And music can be just that. Which music is strictly up to you.

Here is one track which is particularly enticing. If not this, I suggest a track with a steady, rhythmic beat, a strong drum line, and minimal lyrics.

"Eternal Dance," by Gabrielle Roth & The Mirrors. Album is "Music for Slow Flow Yoga." This particular track is slow, rhythmic and lasts nine minutes. You may find you want something faster, or, longer. Find what works best for you so you can feel carried away by the music.

4. Stillness

Start where you are, my love. Just lie down and take a moment to be still.

Remember, stillness does not mean stopping. It actually means making space to get interested in all of that wonderful material moving through you right now: your worries, your joys, the sensations in your body. Make room for all of it. This may be where you stay for the whole practice. It is a beautiful place to be.

5. One Gesture

Did you know that in every moment and in every breath a new cell is born? Did you know that at this very second, you have new biology being created? At this very second, there is a real and tangible new beginning in you.

And that new cell, my love, has not heard all those little self-sabotages you whisper every time you pass the mirror or the worries you have because somehow your body isn't behaving in the way you want it to.

At this very second, you are new. All it takes is one cell. Because that one cell is a manifest, real thing which has ever existed before.

We invite that cell to listen to the music. We let that one cell tell you how to move.

Because that one cell is already dancing with the heartbeat of you. Like the heartbeat of the drum you hear, weaving its rhythm in vibration, so too does your cell weave its rhythm with the beat of your heart.

Hear the pulse of the music, and let your body move just one thing! A finger, a wrist, a leg, your head. It matters not at all what or how you move. Just find one gesture, perhaps in time to the music, and then stay with it. Spend a few minutes letting the gesture get really big, then really small. Get to know that gesture really well.

Then, let it go. Simply let the gesture cease.

6. **Another Gesture**

And so, start again. Listen to the music and let the vibration of the drum call to the vibration of that one, new cell.

Find a gesture. Grow it, shrink it. Know it.

Then let it go.

Rinse and repeat as often as you desire.

This, my love, is Dance. This, my love, is You.

7. **Let Love Move You**

When I first started my own conscious dance practice, I studied with a true master. He helped me wake up even more to my own love of movement and to the joys of being in my own body; it didn't take me long to fall in love with him. Oh, nothing ever happened, but how I longed for connection! It took me a few months to realize that I actually wasn't in love with him (I barely knew him at all). I wanted to be him. In my heart of hearts, I wanted to facilitate and invite people to dance.

Often, when we fall in love – or just become enchanted with an acquaintance – we are drawn to the qualities or behaviors we are craving for ourselves.

It's not a bad thing – it just is what it is.

Even my wonderful, brilliant husband, with whom I was married for all kinds of soul-nourishing reasons, had in him qualities when we first met that I really wanted to feel in myself.

Well guess what? You get to be all that you desire in your dance. In your dance, you get to fall in love with your Self.

HOW DOES LOVE MOVE?

Recently I had the opportunity to work with a young mother who came in because she felt she had lost herself and was burnt out taking care of everyone else. Lisa craved her own autonomy and feeling valued for her own sake.

Just for kicks, we talked about what kind of woman would actually take care of herself first. What kind of woman would be so okay with prioritizing herself she might even be called selfish? It didn't take long for Lisa to say, "Queen." "Ooh. Hmmm. So how might a queen stand? How might she walk? How might she dance?"

Within minutes, Lisa was flying around the room, dipping, and swaying.

While there were plenty of marital and family dynamics to work out, that one dance gave Lisa a real, practical, in-her-body knowing of what it would feel like to put herself first.

Feeling is a way of knowing. So now Lisa has a kind of road map back into what it feels like not to be burnt out. Now when things feel stressful, she can refer to that dance and have a point of reference to see what she wants to get back into.

What makes you come alive?

What lights your fire?

What are you doing when you feel most beautiful?

What are your superpowers?

What makes you feel strong?

When in your life have you felt most passionate?

When do you feel most sensual?

How does this (beautiful, powerful, strong, passionate, sensual, fill in the blank...) you move?

Let Love Move You

You are made of Love.

You are made of stardust and substance.

You are fierce and soft.

You are enormous and small.

You are a miracle of motion and mass.

There is nothing you cannot or should not be.

The whole cosmos resides in your very cells.

When you rob yourself of the full expression of who – and how – you are, you do a disservice to the cosmos.

Weep your tears, scream yourself hoarse from the injustices.

Reach into your belly and womb, and know you are whole.

Every molecule, every cell of your being is infused with the knowing of the world. Be the world.

Come Home.

Come Alive.

This. This is your true body. How do you want to move? How do you want to be?

Ask yourself: How do you want to be touched? When? In what way? Where? On what day? At what hour? Here? There?

Let the information surprise you. And then be surprised again.

You are a vital, dynamic creature. Moment to moment.

Welcome yourself. First, my love, you.

Then, take that gorgeous, complicated creature in hand and introduce her to your friend, you sister, your partner to the world.

But first – always first – you.

When you do, you will find that all the hours of self-criticism become empty and hollow words with no meaning.

You are the most complete expression of all the passion and joy within you.

When you dance authentically, no longer does the size of your thighs matter or the way you look in the mirror. All that moves through you is powerful, joyful, whole.

A WORD ABOUT TOUCH

When you dance, you connect to that part of yourself that is fully yourself and knows (if and) how you want to be touched. By being fully yourself, you are open to true intimacy (because you are being intimate with yourself first and foremost).

Being touched is one of the greatest acts of connection. But it is not just connection with another; it is also connection with the self. When I am touched, it is a direct reference point back to me.

When you open to, and find space for, sustaining interest and compassion for (what is your experience of) yourself, then you are open to that from another.

As you have now just practiced all of this within yourself, what about practicing this with an other?

Feel.

Watch.

Welcome.

Dance.

Start with where the two of you are. (Chapter 4)

Make friends with your biology. (Chapter 5)

Welcome the feeling. (Chapter 6)

Enjoy your bodies. Don't dance yet! Just show up for each other! (Chapter 7)

Start to wake up to sensation. (Chapter 8)

Free the blocks. Find out together your yes and no. (Chapter 9)

Let Love Move You. (Yep, make love!) (Chapter 10, Now)

CHAPTER 11

OBSTACLES

Y ou are awake, alive, and in your body. Congratulations.

And.

When you are awake in your own body, you connect to your true self, and consequently have a clearer sense of what is right for you, and what is wrong.

The Practice of Now is a practice for life. And because it is life, there will be challenges. This chapter is to prepare you for what some of those might be and what you might to do to overcome them. You will explore the various ways you may sabotage or resist your own evolution.

We all live our lives in a risk-averse fashion. It is in our nature to avoid danger and stay safe. And usually to stay safe, we avoid change.

Joe Dispeza describes this beautifully in his book *Getting Over Being Yourself,* in which he describes how our brains exist to keep us alive. When we awake in the morning, our hardworking brains respond, "Good. I am alive." And then the brain looks to see what it did yesterday to achieve that outcome. By nature – by your biology! – you are wired to stay alive and do what you did yesterday.

That is part of why it is so frikkin' awesome you have come this far in the Practice. In some very real way, you faced a pattern determined to stay the same, and instead, you have opened to a new way of being.

But guess what? What is around you has not been engaged in the same process, so there is a good chance that what is around may be determined to bring you back. Why would those in your environment want you to change when it puts them in a sense of danger? They didn't ask to change, right?

Now the good news is that your loved ones will probably be thrilled to have your feelings about your body – and your receptivity to touch, and joy – change. My guess is if you have a partner, s/he will be jumping up and down and doing a happy dance that the two of you can now have more satisfying, frequent connection.

What gets interesting is when the feelings about your body also change your feelings about other aspects of your life.

You may find that your whole relationship and attitude toward the world around you has shifted. You may find that by being in touch with your body, you are in touch with a whole new world of desire. You may find that what you desire – in sensation, quality of touch, and manner of living – is different than anything you've ever felt or explored before. You may find that you want to move at a glacial pace or stand on your head while whistling Dixie.

Whatever! As unique as your body is, so too are your appetites and drives.

This is a beautiful place to be. But it may also be threatening to the old ways.

This is a challenge crossroads.

Do not despair. This is only an opportunity to go deeper into the Practice. How you interact with others - and the world around you - is a chance to stay connected to your authentic Self with Love.

What are some of the ways you may resist or want to stay the way you have been?

FEAR

Facing your fears liberates you.

Consider fear. You know it well. We all do. Whether it is something common and familiar, like the first day at a new school or something darker, more hidden, like abuse or trauma; you know what fear is.

I was forty years old, and it was Halloween. I never really liked the scary images of the season, but that night they were everywhere.

I already spent my whole adult life being just a little bit afraid of dark rooms and especially dark living rooms when I was alone. That Halloween, it was dark. I was alone. There was a witch in the living room.

I was a grownup mom who had just tucked her kids into bed with reassurances that everything was cozy and safe.

Except I didn't believe it. That night, as I paused at the base of the stairs and looked over into the dark living room, I caught myself wanting to squeeze my eyes and race up the stairs. But for some reason, I paused. "All right," I said. "Come out from there. Show yourself. I am ready."

Immediately in my mind's eye, I saw the most horrifying, skeletal witch. I am sure there was flesh falling off and just sockets where eyes should have been. For a brief moment, I froze. Then, I paused and said "All right, then. C'mon. Let's go up the stairs together." And in that moment, something shifted in me – in us. With a sense of total welcome – still a little scared but okay – I turned to climb the eight steps up with my witch.

Miraculously, by the third step, she dissolved.

I do not mean to suggest that every time we meet fear head on, it disappears. But I do suggest that facing your fears – even welcoming them – with kindness and compassion – is the way to begin to change your relationship with them.

It is just like any other feeling you have practiced tolerating. You do not need to marinate in it and hold on to it, but you do need to feel it.

Fear, furthermore, is a particular state which is unlike any other.

JANET FARNSWORTH

If you follow to the fear to its source, you will almost always find at the end of the thread a deep need to survive. I mean, just that – frikkin' survive.

At its face value, the instigator of fear is the drive to preserve life. And as we have discussed, life in its distilled, truest form is Love.

When you can face and shift your relationship to fear, you can face and shift your relationship to Life.

Life is what you want with your body.

At least, it is what you want at some core level for yourself. Your work now is to find what fear is keeping you from that thing.

Last year, I led a retreat with a group of women. We just completed a module of this material – finding and releasing obstacles, and finding and releasing fear.

We went out onto the dry, hot land, deep in the desert to walk. About five minutes in, one woman put her arm out and said urgently, "Wait."

I looked up and saw a snake in the path that half us just walked past and the other half was about to pass.

It was a rattlesnake. My first in the wild.

I almost fainted. At best, my heart rate was through the roof, and I felt a small tremble in my whole body.

The woman with whom I was co-leading (and who was pretty close to the snake) said calmly, "Ah, look, sisters. Look at the deep medicine." She knelt, and only a few feet from the snake, said quietly. "See? It is just stretched out in the sun, not coiled – just taking in the heat."

— 169 —

"Look," my co-leader said.

I held my breath and kept looking a little bit up and to the side. "Nope," my inner voices decreed. "Don't look, and then maybe it won't look at you."

My colleague went on another minute or two (it felt like an hour), but it was long enough for me to think, "Okay. Look." Well, I did, and I could see that the snake was relatively quiet and appeared calm.

We thanked it for its medicine and quietly went past.

My every instinct was not to look – as if by not looking, I could make it disappear. But guess what. It was still there.

Your fears, my love, are similar. You may think by not looking at them, you can make them disappear, but you can't.

And like that rattlesnake, we acknowledge their power and their ability to strike. But we stay calm and allow ourselves to see so we can move on.

What is the fear that keeps you from being in your own body?

What benefit is there to you to not be touched?

We gotta go look for that part of you that doesn't want to be in your body.

When I first married, I realized I had quite conveniently married someone with whom I could on some level safely avoid real physical intimacy. Because of my childhood, I pretty much had made a(n unconscious) decision to never let anyone with whom I was genuinely vulnerable be with my body.

Oh, in college if it was a fling or with someone with whom I knew couldn't really be available, I could go there – but with someone that I loved? That portal had slammed shut when I learned that the person I was most supposed to trust/be vulnerable with – my father – used and hurt me.

I am not saying you have the same story. Not at all. But there is some reason that the situation you are in is better for you than an alternative one.

Don't be confused by the words "better" or "benefit." Think of them rather as markers to begin to explore how the dynamics you are in make sense – even if the sense preserves a world view or a way of being that causes you distress.

RESISTANCE

Do this:

First, identify the area in your relationship with your body which causes you the most distress. Is it feeling overweight? Old? Weak? Is it that you cannot feel your body, or hate what you feel now?

The below questions are more global, but go ahead and insert your particular issue. Sit down in a comfortable seat.

Take three breaths.

Then ask yourself:

Why do I hate this aspect of my body?

What do I gain by hating it? What happens if I love it?

What do I gain by loving it?

What do I lose by loving it?

There is some gain or benefit to you by hating your body. If there weren't, you would already have stopped.

The answers may surprise you.

There is some force that is working to keep you safe, and working effectively.

What is that thing?

Then, once you have asked and answered these questions, you now can know the way forward into your next step.

Do you want to continue? Or is there another way?

Can you re-write the script you are living? Is there a different way to think - and move - forward?

Through the crack, the light shines though.

In your resistance, you find the way.

MY PARTNER IS THE PROBLEM

Sometimes what is right for you is different than what you thought (and so acted on) before. The "You" of Now is not who you have been.

"I changed, but no one else did."

You are feeling better, but what about your family? Your friends? Your co-workers?

What about the world around you?

What if your loved one resists? Even objects?

Laura came to my office because she was exhausted all the time and experiencing periodic bouts of anxiety.

After going through the Practice of Now, she felt invigorated and more in touch with her vitality and ease. She wanted to go out, and to see friends, and even to go back to get a graduate degree.

But her husband, Joe, didn't really like that. He kind of liked her feeling a bit passive, and not complaining or wanting to do more. He put together that her therapy was making her more demanding and announced he wasn't going to watch the kids during her scheduled therapy session.

It was a real crisis for Laura, and she had to work through a lot of guilt and resentment (and hire a babysitter) before she could talk with Joe about how the two of them could accommodate her changes so they both felt safe and supported.

Jill, on the other hand, found her partner Melinda highly distrustful of the changes she saw in Jill as Jill blossomed and let love move her. After some time and more soul inquiry, Jill decided it was better for her to end their relationship rather than continue to compromise herself.

A PARTNER INVITATION

If you would like to invite a loved one to witness your work, show him or her this passage:

Greetings, wonderful partner!

I am here to tell you some awesome news.

Your exceptionally loving and committed beloved has just spent valuable time reading about and learning to practice the steps in this book.

She has done it because she loves you and wants to have a better, richer, more satisfying life which she can share with you.

She has confronted some uncomfortable places in herself that up until now kept her holding back from being totally available to you.

And you love her too, but perhaps have felt that she has more to share – and receive – from the intimacy between you two.

Well I have some exciting news! She is ready to explore and supercharge it all.

She has just gone through a course to connect her to the fabulousness and genius of her body – including knowing how she wants to be touched, and what turns her on.

But here is what you need to know:

She may be different and needs time to know how and in what way she can show up for the two of you.

There may be times she just wants you to touch her softly and times she wants you to just push her up against the wall and take her.

There may be times you feel something different than what she is presenting with.

Stay connected.

Talk to her, share what is in you, tell her what you need.

The exciting news is that you are both working toward better, more satisfying connection!

And if you want to find out more about what you want, take this course too!

YOUR ARE THE RESISTANCE

You have done so much work. Hopefully, somewhere in this process, that work opened you to some joy.

Sometimes, joy is as hard to tolerate as the pain. Sometimes harder. Guilt. Shame.

Stories of being undeserving are more familiar, and so they are more comfortable.

Sometimes you are so used to feeling bad about yourself, it is unsettling to feel good.

What to do when you feel great, and don't know how to handle it?

Practice.

Find your Love Breath. Come into your Ordinary. Scan. Witness. Tolerate the moment. Hold the volcano - but let it erupt with delight.

Stanley was a fifty-two year old software engineer when he started the Practice of Now. He

Jamie was a forty-eight-year-old woman whose children had left the home when she came to the Practice of Now. She warmed to it immediately, soon reevaluated her career, and found her way back to her first love, painting. But when she discovered that she was unhappy with her sex life, it felt too threatening to introduce the topic into her marriage, and she instead chose to not have sex for a while. She and her husband had been married for twenty-six years, and no sex wasn't exactly a new thing.

Before long though, she had an affair, which was sexually gratifying but also emotionally draining. The lies and secrecy took their toll on her marriage, and the affair eventually came out.

Now, I do not advocate any behavior. But what Jamie's story suggests is that we can put off how we feel, but eventually how we feel will probably catch up to us.

Those moments when we feel too flooded by sensation and emotion is the right time to get outside support.

Sometimes we are too much in the feeling to be able to hold it, discern and discriminate, and know how to go forward.

This is exactly the time to find an outside therapist or support system.

There will be times when your own witness will be too clouded by your own past and perceptions to be able to make your way to a genuine connection with yourself. Sometimes there are layers over the layers of the Self which make instinct and intuition cloudy.

The professional or third party becomes not unlike a "third witness" to help you see what is actually you and what is clutter.

In Jamie's case, good communication with her partner and continuously going back to the Practice helped guide her back to Truth, but sometimes professional help is needed.

When we stay connected to the Practice of Now, we can guarantee that we have a technology to find what is most true. And remember: What is true is Love. If you are worried that somehow doing the Practice makes you selfish, remember that what we are aspiring to bring out and through you is simply who you already are. And in the tradition of yoga and tantra, who you already are is Love.

Love does not always look pretty or nice. Would you love your child if she insisted on the keys to the car during an ice storm or a knife to cut herself?

It may be that being loving is setting boundaries or re-organizing priorities, but that is you being you.

The difference between love and selfishness is that love begins as an internal dance. When you are really and truly loving yourself, your behaviors and actions come from that place. Your demands for others are only for what is right for you.

Telling your friend to shut up because she talks too much is not an act of love. Telling your friend you need to take a break because you need some quiet is an act of love.

Can you see the difference?

DISCERNMENT AMIDST THE OBSTACLES

The Now is a complicated, dynamic thing. The more you practice, the more you find. When you stay present and learn to navigate the Now, you find layers and layers of history, interpersonal dynamics, family systems, social and cultural challenges, and blind spots.

In every moment, you are not just who you are but also who you have been and will become. You are the sum of it all. Your DNA holds all of the experience of your ancestors and the code which will guide your descendants.

Think about it: If the whole world exists in this moment, that's an awful lotta material.

How to navigate it all and know what part is doing the leading? Is it the truth of your soul's evolution and your best Self, or is it the truth of where you have been and what injuries you have suffered? Your mind!

The Mind

We need the mind. Without it, you wouldn't have known how to identify your problems and navigate the solutions. Take this book, for example. It is the mind that connected the words with your experience and the mind that knew how to pick it up and read it. It will be your mind that will help you figure out how to implement it – when, in what circumstances, and how.

During this process and practice, we instruct the mind to take a break. Well, it is time to bring it back.

We need the mind in the Practice of Now. We need the mind to understand all of the gloriously complex and compacted threads that make up the tapestry of Now.

We need it to learn the art of discrimination and discernment.

Remember my story?

When dance first woke me up, I was a flood of feeling. I wasn't a river of sensation; I was drowning in a tsunami of it.

And the only way I could begin to discern what was was by using my mind. In my case, it was the exceptional therapist with whom I had been working already who helped me understand the storms of feeling I was experiencing.

Like Beth, who we learned about earlier. Beth knew she had learned to hate her body every time her father told her she was fat (when she was an active athlete), but she needed therapy to help connect the ways those experiences were affecting her current choices and relationships.

We can do it on our own but having a third party can make all the difference.

By definition, we can't know what we don't know!

This could be a time to find someone to be compassionately present with no personal agenda, but who can help you not identify with feeling but to feel it and then discriminate out choices about what to do with them.

This Practice will always guide you back to you. Sometimes it's helpful to have support while you are being guided.

ALONE TO ALL ONE

The Practice of Now in its most distilled state is a personal one. You cannot be with anyone in true integrity until you know how to be with yourself first.

But you do not live in a vacuum.

How do you do the Practice when you open the door and interact with others and the world around you?

Vinn Marti of Soul Motion talks about "one eye in and one eye out," to suggest that you learn to stay connected to your interior while connecting to what – and who! – is in your exterior.

You practice letting love move you while you move with others.

Another way to do this is to practice quite literally in community.

I have the great gift of holding a women's circle called the Red Tent once a month. During our meeting, we gather in a circle and simply share what is in our hearts.

When a sister is talking, the rest of us simply listen and witness. There is no cross talk, no need to reassure or advise.

As women, we are so entrained to take care of and interact with another's experience that sometimes we forget that all we need – all the answers, all the wisdom and strength – is already inside each one of us.

The Red Tent is also a powerful antidote to the impulse to perform. There is a contract that what is shared in the Tent stays in the Tent, and in fact, this includes even fixing on anything a sister says beyond the time we are together. What is said one need not be what wants to be said again.

With no pressure to be anything other than what are, we discover a freedom to express ourselves authentically. By feeling freed from advice, analysis, or even time, we discover the power of being in the Now as our true Selves.

The final way, of course, to practice this next step is to dance in community.

Dancing with others becomes a potent way to renegotiate how to be in society as yourself.

CHAPTER 12

ABUNDANCE AHEAD

Y our body is not just an expression of you, it is you. This is a book about connecting you to the genius of your body, and so by definition, to the genius of you.

And so let us remind you one more time: who you are is already fierce, funny, strong, vulnerable, smart, silly, hot, sexy, voluptuous, and oh-so-alive!

The shape, size, and appearance of your body is a mere holder of what is inside. What is inside is wise and powerful.

You began this journey struggling with your body – how it looked, what it felt like, how your relationship with it affected your life.

In the Practice of Now, you paused the fight, and hopefully found a friend.

What was a battleground is now beautiful.

With this practice, you can now know that you are divinity in body.

I used to always contract a bit when someone would call herself, or call me, a goddess. I always thought that was a bit sacrilegious. It was so much a part of my belief system to defer to what is sacred. I still do – very much.

As I do this practice more and more, I find I can accept that I can access the divine, and find Spirit within – not just outside – of me.

Inside of you there is treasure cove of jewels. Inside, there are riches of fortitude and vulnerability, of wisdom and humor. There is the absolute knowing of how to be touched, and how to give and receive pleasure. There is the deep, gut knowing of what is right, and what is wrong. There is You.

Whatever you call that thing, that thing which animates you, how do you connect?

At the very least, how do you access that energy? How do you communicate with Spirit or hear Spirit communicate with you? That relationship is so personal. It is within. Everything you perceive – and know – you perceive through the lens of your own mind, your own feelings, your own senses.

Your own experiences.

And how do you define and know your own experiences?

You access all of it through the knowing of your body. In a very real way, your connection with the body gives you an almost divine connection to, and authorship over, the universe of you.

THE PRACTICE OF NOW: LET LOVE MOVE YOU

Take this practice. Explore it. Refine it. Challenge it. Chew it. Tease it. Dance it. Know it.

It is yours. It can never be anything other than yours because all it seeks to do is to connect you to you.

Everything in this book is just an offering. I share with you through the lens of my own experience, my own body. The only truth is your own.

Use these steps not as rigid rights, but as guideposts to bring you back to you. Re-shape them, expand on them, edit or embellish. They are now yours.

Step One: Know – truly know – that all progress, evolution and joy begins (and ends) with you.

In order to be open to pleasure, you need to be open to you.

Step Two: (Make Friends with) Your Biology

Become comfortable in your own (actual) skin. How? Learn how to know – and not judge! – your body. Your biology is an intelligent system and offers important information to understand who you are.

Your body and biology are who you are, and who you are is perfect.

Step Three: Know Your Heart

Now that you are connected to your biology, connect to the feeling which flows through it.

Feeling is both in the body and in the heart, and you need to learn how to connect to both.

Step Four: Your Body Is the Beginning

Use practical skills how to be in, and feel, the body and heart as the first step to banish the blame, and instead, feel vital and creative.

Use the art of breathing to access compassion. Anchor into the ordinary with a body scan to learn how to tolerate, sustain, and welcome sensation. Then learn to explore the body as a landscape and playground, with movement analysis.

Step Five: Awaken Your Body to Its Own Sensual Pleasures

Turn on and light up the natural energetic centers in your body as a way to connect to pleasure. The power of personal movement clarifies and connects you to your natural instincts, and your natural instincts know how to bring you back to the experience of Love (and love for your Self!).

Step Six: Access your Intuition. (And Before Taking That Final Dive into Surrender, Know What Is Keeping You Back).

Further, honor and recognize any ways that the "keeping you back" also might come from wisdom. Learn to know your "yes" and "no."

Step Seven: At Last, Dance

You now know specific techniques to begin spontaneous and genuine movement as an expression of you. You understand that dance is a method of expressing yourself honestly, personally, powerfully, and joyfully. When you dance, you connect to that part of you that is fully yourself and knows just how beautiful you are.

Beautiful Being, you now know how to honor your body and also how to connect to your body as a vibrant tool to feel more vital, creative, and peaceful.

Use this book as a map back home to you. When you get there, you will remember the most magnificent places – the joys you came into the world knowing. The pleasure of sight and sound and taste and smell. You will remember the beautiful, complicated, and gloriously alive world of your feeling. You will remember you.

My wish for you is to never forget how magnificent you are and to know that you truly are a miracle in motion.

Treat that miracle with the reverence it deserves. Blessings on your journey.

The Practice of Now: Let Love Move You

ACKNOWLEDGMENTS

I resisted writing this for a long while, as it felt like expressing thanks to specific people by definition meant I was being silent about others.

So if you are not mentioned below, please know from the bottom of my heart that this doesn't mean I have forgotten about you, or that I am not grateful. In fact, that you are reading this at all guarantees my profound thanks.

To those I name, I want to thank the entire team at The Author's Way: Dr Angela Lauria, for seeing it all, and being the gateway through which we all pass. Cheyenne, for your extraordinary mix of utter gentility and Mama-bear sized organization. (I shall see you in your perfectly appointed, clean beach house!) Mehrina, for your always kind patience as you guided me through my enormously wobbly first steps. Ramses, for, well, everything. Your coaching quite simply changed my life. And to the delightful Cory, whose easy laughter and big heart almost obscured the rigorous editing and hard paces you walked with me. Thank you to everyone (and remember, to those whose names I do not know) at The Castle!

To my first teacher, Jackie Walker, the first Soul I learned to trust. You were then, as you are now, my Earth Angel.

To my greatest teacher, Lydia Salant. This book, quite simply, would not exist without you. More than that, in a very real way *I* would not exist without you; the awakened Self I so gratefully inhabit became available only inside the beautiful arms you held so wide, and in the wisdom you shared.

To my constant teachers: My students and clients. Some of you will recognize yourselves in the stories I tell in this book; others will wonder where you are. I promise you: You are in every word. Every step we took together, every victory you won, you have inspired me more than you can ever imagine. I could not 'know' what I do without the courage and grace of your practice. And to Soma Vida and Sukha studios especially, I am so honored to be a part of the special tribes you are! Thank you, thank you, thank you.

To Joss Price, who taught me one of the best lessons of all: How to love, and love with integrity. We went through a lot, and I am beyond grateful to have you as my best friend.

To Ward Farnsworth, whose name I still proudly share. How to even quantify or identify the countless ways you have made my life better? We may live on different tracks, but my heart will always travel with you.

Finally, to Sam and Annie. YOU. ARE. THE. BEST. KIDS. EVER. Period. I am so proud of you. I see who you are becoming, and I am in awe. Please, always stay you. Never be anyone other than the fierce, funny, smart, beautiful, kind, magnificent Souls you are. It is an honor to be your mom. I love you forever.

THANK YOU

From the bottom of my heart: Thank you for reading this book.

These pages hold journeys of a life time, and I am so honored to able to share them with you.

Somewhere not too far below the surface, I can feel my inner eleven-year-old, still sitting on her bedroom floor, surrounded by a pile of books, and daydreaming about someday being an author. And while she didn't know what to call it, she was also daydreaming about trying to do something that mattered, something that came from her Soul. This book is the realization of those dreams.

It astounds me it is in your hands.

I recognize your time is precious, and that you spent some of it to pick up this book delights and awes me.

As a gesture of appreciation and in honor of your time, I would like to give you a free recorded version of the Body Scan section of this book so you don't have to remember the instructions (and so avoid that read, peek, practice, read, peek, practice, repeat thing…. and so on)!

Please email me at JanetFarnsworth@Yahoo.com and just write "Bring me home, Janet!" in the subject line, and I will send you the MP3.

Contact me www.janetfarnsworth.com for any further questions, or if you would like to chat more about The Practice of Now: Let Love Move You. In all things, Love On!

ABOUT THE AUTHOR

J ANET FARNSWORTH, nationally recognized yoga teacher and body-empowerment coach, inspires students to break through old beliefs of shame and blame, and instead connect to their bodies as the source of their greatest wisdom and joy.

Janet created The Practice of Now: Let Love Move You, a movement therapy practice designed to heal and nurture our relationships with our bodies. She believes authentic movement is the fastest way to physical and emotional spiritual health and well-being.

With a graduate degree in social work, Janet also brings a background in expressive therapy, psychodrama, ecstatic dance, and yoga.

Her book, Love Your Body: The Ultimate Guide to Stop Making Your Body a Battleground, is a how-to for anyone who is ready to feel empowered and at peace with their body.

Janet currently resides in Austin, Texas, where she is proud to be a part of Conviction Yoga, a program to bring the healing arts of yoga to incarcerated men and women.

A personal survivor of the blame game, she enjoys the challenge of finding ways to wake up each morning and be glad to be in the body she actually has, particularly the stretch marks on her stomach and the cellulite on her thighs.

When she is not trying to hug her almost-adult children, Janet loves being on any boat, watching old movies, and eating buttered toast (either one at a time, or all at once).

ABOUT DIFFERENCE PRESS

Difference Press is the exclusive publishing arm of The Author Incubator, an educational company for entrepreneurs – including life coaches, healers, consultants, and community leaders – looking for a comprehensive solution to get their books written, published, and promoted. Its founder, Dr. Angela Lauria, has been bringing to life the literary ventures of hundreds of authors-in-transformation since 1994.

A boutique-style self-publishing service for clients of The Author Incubator, Difference Press boasts a fair and easy-to-understand profit structure, low-priced author copies, and author-friendly contract terms. Most importantly, all of our #incubatedauthors maintain ownership of their copyright at all times.

LET'S START A MOVEMENT WITH YOUR MESSAGE

In a market where hundreds of thousands of books are published every year and are never heard from again, The Author Incubator is different. Not only do all Difference Press books reach Amazon bestseller status, but all of our authors are actively changing lives and making a difference.

Since launching in 2013, we've served over 500 authors who came to us with an idea for a book and were able to write it and get it self-published in less than 6 months. In addition, more than 100 of those books were picked up by traditional publishers and are now available in book stores. We do this by selecting the highest quality and highest potential applicants for our future programs.

Our program doesn't only teach you how to write a book – our team of coaches, developmental editors, copy editors, art directors, and marketing experts incubate you from having a book idea to being a published, bestselling author, ensuring that the book you create can actually make a difference in the world. Then we give you the training you need to use your book to make the difference in the world, or to create a business out of serving your readers.

ARE YOU READY TO MAKE A DIFFERENCE?

You've seen other people make a difference with a book. Now it's your turn. If you are ready to stop watching and start taking massive action, go to http://theauthorincubator.com/apply/ .

"Yes, I'm ready!"

OTHER BOOKS BY
DIFFERENCE PRESS

Going Home: Saying Goodbye with Grace and Joy When You Know Your Time is Short by Michael G. Giovanni, Jr.

Get Happier, Fitter, and off the Meds Now!: 7-Steps to Improved Health and a Body You Love by Ell Graniel

Healed: A Divinely Inspired Path to Overcoming Cancer by Pamela Herzer, M.A.

Live Healthy With Hashimoto's Disease: The Natural Ayurvedic Approach to Managing Your Autoimmune Disorder by Vikki Hibberd

I Left My Toxic Relationship – Now What?: The Step-By-Step Guide to Starting over and Living on Your Own by Heather J. Kent

Sign Your First Coaching Client: Steps to Launch Your New Career by Carine Kindinger

Find Your Beloved: Your Guide to Attract True Love by Rosine Kushnick

My Toddler Has Stopped Having so Many Tantrums: The Mother's Guide to Finding Joy in Parenting by Susan Jungermann

In the Eye of a Relationship Storm: Know What to Do in an Abusive Situation by Jackquline Ann

My Clothes Fit Again!: The Overworked Women's Guide to Losing Weight by Sue Seal

How Do I Survive?: 7 Steps to Living After Child Loss by Patricia Sheveland

Your Life Matters: Learn to Write Your Memoir in 8 Easy Steps by Junie Swadron

Medication Detox: How to Live Your Best Health, Simplified by Rachel Reinhart Taylor, M.D.

Keeping Well: An Anti-Cancer Guide to Remain in Remission by Brittany Wisniewski